D1431816

Mackinac

ILLINOIS PRAIRIE DPL

A65501 992592

Mackinac

by
Donna Marie Lively

TOURIST TOWN GUIDES™

ILLINOIS PRAIRIE DISTRICT LIBRARY

917.
7404
LIV

Mackinac (*Tourist Town Guides*™ series)
© 2009 by Donna Marie Lively

Published by:
Channel Lake, Inc., P.O. Box 1771, New York, NY 10156-1771
http://www.channellake.com

Author: Donna Marie Lively
Editors: Elisa Lee, Dirk Vanderwilt
Cover Design: Julianna Lee
Cover Photos: Ellen Lively

Published in April, 2009

All rights reserved. Published in the United States of America. No part of this book may be reproduced in any form or by any means without permission in writing from the publisher. *Tourist Town Guides*™ is a trademark of Channel Lake, Inc. All other trademarks and service marks are the properties of their respective owners.

ISBN-13: 978-0-9767064-7-2

Disclaimer: The information in this book has been checked for accuracy. However, neither the publisher nor the author may be held liable for errors or omissions. *Use this book at your own risk.* To obtain the latest information, we recommend that you contact the vendors directly. If you do find an error, let us know at corrections@channellake.com.

Channel Lake, Inc. is not affiliated with the vendors mentioned in this book, and the vendors have not authorized, approved or endorsed the information contained herein. This book contains the opinions of the author, and your experience may vary.

917.7404

For more information, visit http://www.touristtown.com

Help Our Environment!

Even when on vacation, your responsibility to protect the environment does not end. Here are some ways you can help our planet without spoiling your fun:

✓ Ask your hotel staff not to clean your towels and bed linens each day. This reduces water waste and detergent pollution.

✓ Turn off the lights, heater, and/or air conditioner when you leave your hotel room.

✓ Use public transportation when available. Tourist trolleys are very popular, and they are usually cheaper and easier than a car.

✓ Recycle everything you can, and properly dispose of rubbish in labeled receptacles.

Tourist towns consume a lot of energy. Have fun, but don't be wasteful. Please do your part to ensure that these attractions are around for future generations to visit and enjoy.

Dedicated to Craig, Ellen, Matthew and Olivia for their unending support and love of exploration.

Special acknowledgment and thanks to Marilyn and Jennifer for believing and taking risks.

COVER IMAGES
Front Cover: The Grand Hotel *(© Ellen Lively)*, the Mackinac Bridge *(© Ellen Lively)*, and the Father Marquette Memorial *(© Ellen Lively)*. *Back Cover:* Arch Rock *(© Ellen Lively)*.

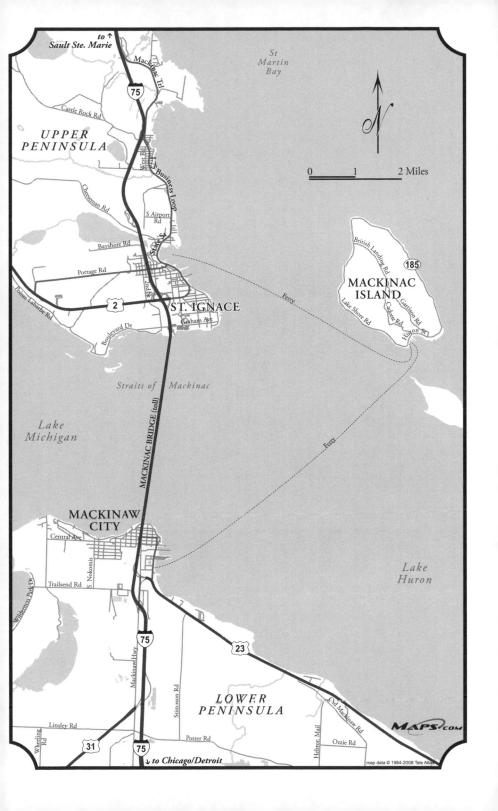

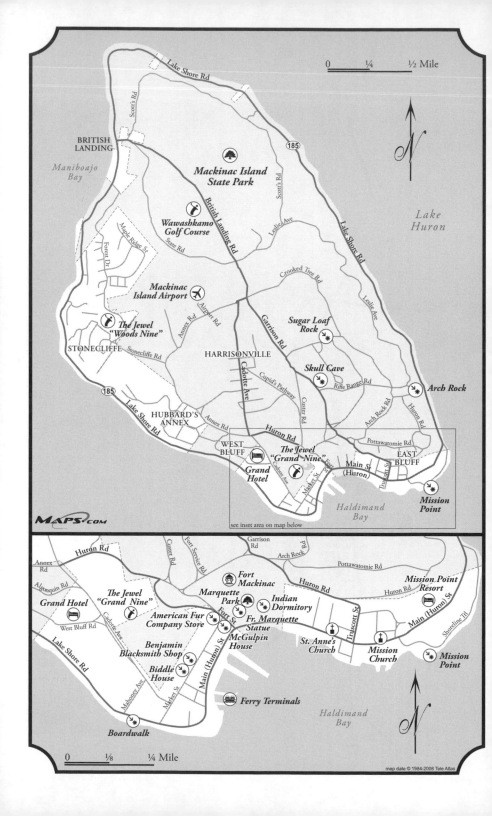

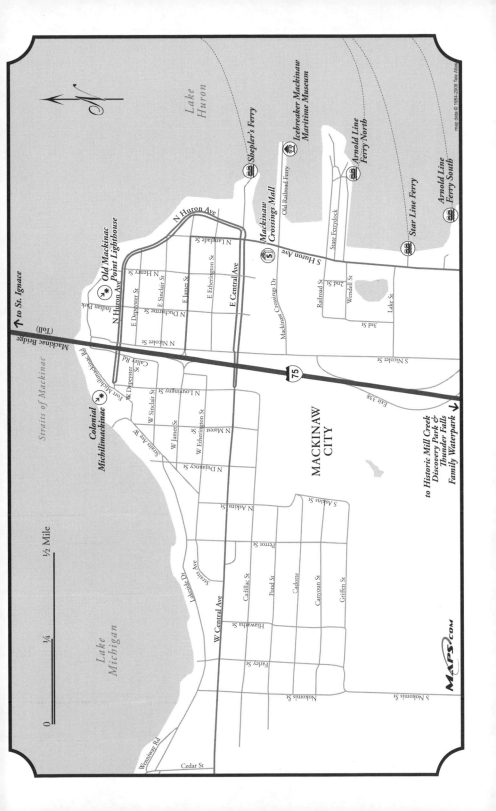

Table of Contents

Introduction 15

    How to Use this Book   *16*

Mackinac History 19

    Early Inhabitants   *19*
    The Explorers   *21*

The Mackinac Bridge 35

Area Orientation 41

    Visiting Mackinac   *43*
    Arriving By Land   *46*
    Air Travel   *48*
    Getting to Mackinac Island by Sea   *49*
    Marinas   *51*
    Getting Around Mackinaw City   *52*

Mackinac Island Transportation 55

    Getting Around Mackinac Island   *60*

Seasons and Events 65

    Summer   *65*
    Fall   *68*
    Winter   *70*
    Spring   *71*

Mackinac Island State Park 73

    Mackinac State Historic Parks   *74*
    Other Historic Sites   *79*
    The War of 1812 Sites   *80*
    Mackinac Rock Formations   *82*

Mackinaw City Attractions 93

    Historic Mackinaw City   *93*

Mackinaw City Water Fun   *95*
Mackinaw City Attractions   *97*
Parks Near Mackinaw City   *99*

Other Attractions **105**

Mackinac Island   *105*
Golf   *107*

Shopping.. **111**

Mackinaw City   *112*
Mackinac Island   *116*

Dining **119**

Mackinaw City   *120*
Mackinac Island   *126*

Mackinaw City Accommodations............................... **135**

Waterpark Hotels   *135*
Hotels and Motels   *137*
Bed and Breakfasts   *143*
Campgrounds   *144*

Mackinac Island Accommodations............................. **147**

Resorts   *147*
Hotels and Motels   *149*
Bed and Breakfasts   *153*

Day Trips.. **157**

Sault Ste. Marie   *157*
St. Ignace   *162*
Northern Lake Michigan   *165*
South Mackinac   *167*

Recommendations **171**

Index **175**

Did you know... ?

Colonial Michilimackinac is the longest active archaeological dig in the United States.

Introduction

On **Mackinac Island** – a tiny island near where Lake Huron joins Lake Michigan – time almost seems to stand still. People travel by bicycle and horse-drawn carriage, the streets are clean, the parks are abundant, hotels are luxurious, shops are small and residents are friendly. It is a place as calm and peaceful as it is vibrant and inviting. It is widely respected as the "Crown Jewel of Michigan," and with good cause.

Part of the *Straits of Mackinac*, it is no surprise that Mackinac draws more tourists than any other place in Michigan. One of several islands in the straits, Mackinac Island is certainly not the largest. The cause of its regency lies not in its size, but in the many secrets it holds. It is the custodian of sacred legends and history, marking events that date from the beginning of time. No other island in the area has exerted such power over the imaginations and lives of people.

The island's location in the straits gains weather protection by the guardian peninsulas. It still snows and blows here, but more gently than on some of the other nearby sentinels. Winds that scour other places are tamed into precision tools to sculpt the island's limestone into structures. This geology and protection have styled the island with an array of ecosystems that flourish. An amazing gathering of flora, from tree varieties to tapestry carpets of flowers, graces this island as in few other places of the world. Concerning the wild things, birds find that holding court at Mackinac Island is ideal. Rare and endangered species find refuge here. This one small island, only eight miles in circumference, believes in the importance of every guest, human and animal alike.

Nearby **Mackinaw City**, on the north tip of Michigan's Lower Peninsula, has its own story to tell. It has grown from a neglected, wind-swept sandy plain into a welcoming, rejuvenating refuge. It is a planned city that has dreamed and fought for each step of its growth. Mackinaw City has gone through many changes and experiments before becoming comfortable with its identity. Those changes and experiments are wonderful fireside stories now. They tell of courage, determination, frustration and humor. Ask around and you may hear them shared by the descendants of those who lived through the tales.

Today, Mackinaw City has recognized and embraced its role as a stopover en route to Mackinac Island. The earliest accounts characterize Mackinaw City as a place to rest before continuing the journey at hand. It relishes this heritage as the "gathering place."

HOW TO USE THIS BOOK

Attractions in this book may have an address, website (🖰), and/or telephone number (☎). Some items have other items within them (for example, a restaurant within a hotel). Sometimes the contact information may be with the inline text, or there may be no contact information. If there is no contact information, please see the attraction or section heading.

Must-See Attractions: Headlining must-see attractions, or those that are otherwise iconic or defining, are designated with the 🏛 symbol. The author and/or editor made these and all other qualitative value judgments.

Coverage: This book is not all-inclusive. It is comprehensive, with many different options for entertainment, dining, eating, shopping, etc., but there are many establishments not listed here. Since this is an independent guide, the decision of what to include was made entirely by the author and/or editor.

Attraction Pricing: When applicable, at the end of each attraction listing is a general pricing reference, indicated by dollar signs, relative to other attractions in the region. The scale is from "$" (least expensive) to "$$$$" (most expensive). Contact the attraction directly for specific pricing information. **Please note that** if the attraction is free, or if no pricing information is available at the time of publication, or if a price indication is otherwise irrelevant, then the dollar sign scale is omitted from the listing.

"Family Friendly" Designations: This book mentions attractions that may have a "family friendly" attitude. *However,* this does *not* guarantee that the attraction meets any kind of standards for you or your family. It is merely an opinion that the attraction is generally appropriate for children. You are urged to contact all establishments directly for further information.

Mackinac History

Long before the incorporation of Mackinaw City, prehistoric fishing camps had dotted the area. Exactly who they were has not yet been determined. Certainly, they were the forerunners of the Native American presence that would claim the area some 700 years before the arrival of the Europeans.

EARLY INHABITANTS

Winters have always been hard in the Mackinac area. Even as the frigidity of the glacial age passed, family groups were linking themselves into larger bands and forming what came to be called tribes. As the climate became more temperate, permanent villages were established. The tribes began to build coalitions, and nations were born. Linked by similar lifestyles, tribes maintained their identities through clothing style, traditions and practicing distinct customs.

Language became the foundation of distinguishing the tribes into their various nations. Two main language groups belong to the western Great Lakes area: the Algonquin and the Siouan. Rivalry between the groups forced the Siouan speaking tribes into the most western parts of the area. Eventually, large portions of these groups ranged into Wisconsin, Minnesota and the Great Plains.

Faced with continued warfare and the encroachment of warring tribes from the east, three Algonquin tribes borrowed a style of government from their rivals, the Iroquois. Their willingness to adapt themselves to new ideas, regardless of the source, speaks of their determination to survive and to survive well. The Anishinabe, the Potawatomi and the Odawa formed a covenant and became known as the "Three Fires." They were so closely related that they considered themselves as older, middle and younger brothers. This bond has played a crucial part in the history of the Mackinac area. Their unity still thrives today, assuring their role into the future.

For the nations of the Three Fires and many others, Mackinac Island was viewed as an especially holy place. It was the site of offerings, vision quests and other activities appropriate to the home of the Great Manitoulin. Mackinac Island also has the distinction of being the final resting place for important tribal leaders. Because of this, the Island was not a battleground among the Native Americans. It is considered to be the land of the Great Turtle, a character in Native mythology that carries the world on his back. The shape of the island roughly resembles a turtle and so was an easy landmark for the original nations.

ANISHINABE

"Anishinabe" is the name that they gave themselves. It is translated simply as "the people," a modest moniker for one of the area's largest nations. Various other names have been attached to this group. They were also known as the Ojibwe, the Ojibway and the Chippewa. They claimed the area north and south of Lake Superior (the Upper Peninsula) and north of Lake Huron. They survived on hunting, fishing and gathering of natural crops, primarily wild rice. Wild rice is the grain of natural grasses that grow in the swampy areas at the edges of lakes.

POTAWATOMI

The Potawatomi, or Weshnabek, tribe was generally situated south of the Straits of Mackinac, filling the area between Lake Michigan and Lake Huron. Other groups gave this name to them, which means "people of the fire," referring to the brilliant pottery they crafted from clay in their area. The Potawatomi cultured crops, such as tobacco and healing herbs, alongside their food. They tended to be a quiet people, enjoying their lifestyle of fishing, hunting, growing and creating. Their own appellation of "Weshnabek," or "the people," reflects humility and satisfaction.

ODAWA

Of the three nations, the Ottawa, or Odawa, nation was possibly the most adventurous. Their name means "at-home-anywhere-people" or "to trade." This makes them the obvious ones to welcome the newcomers from Europe. Prior to that meeting, however, the Odawa traded with other native nations from all over the continent. They made their home base on the eastern shores of Lake Huron as well as the many islands in the area. Archaeologists have unearthed their camps on Mackinac Island and nearby Manitoulin Island. Their legends in particular have come down to us as the first history of Mackinac Island and the Straits of Mackinac.

THE EXPLORERS

Exactly when the first people crossed the Atlantic Ocean is a mystery. The Vikings tried to settle on the east coast as early as 900 AD. While the settlement failed, the door for limited contact with the New World was opened.

While the Spanish left their mark on South America, Mexico and the southern part of North America, the British were making tentative inroads on the middle section of the east coast. With less fanfare, the French were exploring part of the northern territory. King Francis I of France commissioned Giovanni da Verrazano to explore the American coastline in 1524. Six years later, the King sent Jacques Cartier on a mission to North America.

JACQUES CARTIER, 1530

Jacques Cartier sailed from France in April 1534 to chart a northwest passage through North America to China. Instead, he encountered the Gulf of St. Lawrence. He also realized the importance and the viability of French settlements in this New World. One discovery made it into his reports although he does not seem to have grasped its significance at the time: beaver pelts.

Beaver pelts were abundant in the Native American house-holds and dress. This would become the "gold" of the North American continent that most Europeans were seeking. This find was not significant in 1534, but by the early 1600s the beaver populations in Europe would be all but exterminated. The desire for these furs would increase as would the value of each pelt. The loss of European beaver would bring dramatic change to the distant Mackinac gathering place.

SAMUEL CHAMPLAIN, 1603

In 1603, Samuel Champlain was commissioned to join Francois Grave du Pont on an expedition to North America. His assignment as pilot was to make detailed notes and maps for King Henri of France. As further and further into the rivers and forests he went, he established settlements. He founded Quebec in 1608. It would be from Quebec that the North American fur trade would fan out and cover an entire continent. By 1616, Samuel Champlain was too distracted with governing the new settlements to continue exploring. Two young men stepped in to fill the gap.

ETIENNE BRULE AND JEAN NICOLET, 1618

Etienne Brule is the first recorded individual to be designated as a coureur de bois. Literally translated, this means "runner of the woods." He had arrived with Champlain as a teenager in 1608. Champlain sent him to live with the Algonquins in order to learn their ways. Etienne Brule never fully returned to the European life-style. He was quite literally a "runner of the woods." His travels took him farther into the continent than any other white man had gone. Historians believe that he was the first European to see Lake Huron. His exploits opened the way west to many others.

Jean Nicolet arrived in New France in 1618. He became one of the official French interpreters. The life of a coureur de bois suited him well. He was the first Frenchman to explore as far as

Wisconsin. He was most likely the first of his nation to see Mackinac Island and the land that would become Mackinaw City.

COUREURS DE BOIS AND VOYAGEURS

As more and more men followed the path of the coureur de bois, valuable animal pelts began to arrive in the settlements. These were traded for supplies. As the industry progressed, voyageurs became an integral link in the transfer of pelts. These "water men" specialized in handling large canoes that could carry tons of cargo. Fearlessly (or so it seemed) they paddled across the Great Lakes, portaged around rapids and waterfalls risking death many times a day. The Native inhabitants taught them well. As with the coureurs de bois, many of the voyageurs lived lives that embraced the Native American culture. Over the next two centuries, millions of dollars worth of beaver belts would pass through Mackinac on their way to Quebec and then Europe.

THE JESUITS ARRIVE

The fur traders were not the only ones roaming the woods. Jesuit priests of the Roman Catholic Church arrived committed to exploration and converting the Native Americans. Their habit of recording their work and discoveries has been invaluable to both their contemporaries and modern historians. In 1668, Father Jacques Marquette and Father Claude Dablon established a small mission on the rapids of the St. Mary's River to reach the northern tribes. It was the first permanent European settlement in Michigan and the Mid-west: Sault Ste. Marie. Father Marquette later built a chapel on Mackinac Island before choosing St. Ignace on the northern side of the straits as his permanent base. From here he conducted his amazing explorations with Louis Jolliet that included reaching the Mississippi River.

THE FIRST EUROPEANS TO GATHER AT MICHILIMACKINAC

In 1669, Adrien Jolliet visited the Lower Peninsula of Michigan. He is believed to be the first European to do so. As the older brother of the more renowned Louis Jolliet, he deserves this mention. When he stepped onto the shores of the south side of the straits, it was enough to begin the steady flow of French to the area. Fur trading was now the main business of New France. The Mackinac area proved to be the key link in the efficient exportation of the tons of fur that would soon become available.

THE BRITISH MAKE THEIR MOVE

The British established the Hudson Bay Company in 1690 to try to garner a piece of this rich commodity and to break the French monopoly. They laid claim to the entire drainage basin of the Hudson Bay. This effectively put them in bitter competition with the French. The French responded by racing towards the Mississippi River with a string of forts built to protect their fur claims and territory. Joining this line of defense in 1715 was Fort Michilimackinac on the tip of the Lower Peninsula of Michigan.

Native Americans viewed the new fort and its contingent of soldiers with raised eyebrows. The French inhabitants welcomed the greater official recognition. The inhabitants of Michilimackinac settled back into their pleasant habit of exchanging trade, cultures and life. The respect they had for each other wasn't always perfectly harmonious, of course, but it was well enough established for the groups to continue in mutually beneficial existence.

WAR!

A series of wars between the French and English began. The short lulls between conflicts saw the Mackinac based fur trade maintaining its prosperity. Mackinac Island continued its reign as a Native American holy sanctuary. It was pretty much business as usual at the historic gathering place. The Straits of Mackinac were used to change.

France's primary disadvantage was its focus on commerce via the fur trade and not on settlements. This meant that France had a smaller populace from which to build a militia. Their military had to be brought almost entirely from Europe. France's primary asset was its relationship with the Native Americans.

While France was thus engaged, England had been busy establishing settlements. As the settlements grew, this effectively produced a homegrown militia vitally interested in the outcome of any conflict. The spats continued between the two superpowers. The truce that followed them was simply a pause for breath before the main event.

THE FRENCH AND INDIAN WAR

It began in 1753 with early success for the British. Their fortune turned as the British incompetence in forest warfare was displayed. The forced but bloodless surrender of Fort Necessity by a young George Washington set the final test of wills in place. Only the Iroquois Confederation aligned itself with the British. This was a gift to the French. Since almost every remaining tribe was a sworn enemy of the Iroquois with a long list of grievances, France found its native militia ready and willing. They fought for ten bloody years.

By 1760, Quebec and Detroit were in the hands of British forces. A year later, Montreal was in the same position. Finally, in 1763, a worn out France met with England and signed the Treaty of Paris. She gave England her colonies in India, Canada and all possessions east of the Mississippi, north of Florida. She had already handed the Louisiana territory over to Spain in a gesture of appreciation for Spain's loyalty and alliance. With the stroke of a pen, France's dominance in Mackinac and the world came to an end. The empire that England had long dreamed of now lay at her feet.

BRITISH RULE

It had been a costly war. France was left with a war debt that ate up half of the annual budget just to pay the interest. The coveted beaver pelt trade had slipped through her fingers. She had lost vast territories and her place on the world stage.

England's victory had been purchased with monumental debt. Of far more importance to her North American colonies was the cost in life and property. Many families never recovered. Their attitude towards their motherland began to change. Britain's attitude towards the colonies changed as well. The colonists were viewed as a burden. Many in England felt that they were not paying their "fair" share of the economic upheaval. Britain's rule became harsher and more demanding.

For the former citizens of New France, this distant tyrant was tolerated while a deep-seeded anger simmered. But the Native Americans, more than the rest, despised the new order of things. They had lost the most in the war; families, homes, homeland, ancient tribal alliances and any remnant of respect that they had engendered with the Europeans. The British lorded their victory over the trade industry and everything else. Particularly with the Native Americans, trade goods were limited or disappeared entirely. The tribes had long ago become dependent on guns for warfare and to support their families. The regulation of these goods brought continued loss to native homes as food supplies were more difficult to gain. Out of this smoldering powder keg of animosity, arose an Ottawa leader. His name was Pontiac.

PONTIAC'S WAR

Pontiac was born into the tribe of the "at-home-anywhere" people. He took this concept to a new level for the Native Americans. He traded on their feelings of abandonment and resentment to build a coalition previously unknown among the native nations. His home was anywhere that he could find a common bond against the British. He was powerful in build and marked with the extraordinary tattooed markings of his people. This only added mystique to his unusual oratory skills. Pontiac, a chief among the Ottawas, quickly became a chief among many tribes. Even the Iroquois Confederation joined him in his plot to destroy the English. His plan was simple. Tribes would infiltrate and overrun the forts in their area. Those that had not been killed would be driven from their lands and Native American rule would be restored. It was to be orchestrated on the same day so that forts could not come to the aid of one another. There would be strength in unity. He was right.

MASSACRE AT MICHILIMACKINAC

The spring of 1763 had arrived. The little dock at Fort Michilimackinac was fairly bursting with the comings and goings. Voyageurs' paddles kept rhythm to their boisterous songs. Tribes from all over the north kept arriving. Those that had arrived early on had witnessed the turning over of the fort into British hands. It appeared to be business as usual. A Jewish trader by the name of Ezekiel Solomon set up business at Michilimackinac. He is noted as the first Jewish settler in Michigan. Young Alexander Henry came, too. He was the first British trader to settle at the fort. This was a bold move considering the general hostility and distrust harbored for English businessmen. Henry pushed on and won friends among every group assembled at the straits. He was adopted by a local chieftain, Chief Wawatam, in response to a vision that the chief had seen years before. Alexander Henry recorded all of this in his diary. Dramatic changes had happened, but the fur trade remained profitable and life at Mackinac was looking as good as ever.

June 2, 1763 dawned bright and clear. By all accounts it was a warm day, especially for this early in the season. Yet no one took notice of the native women wrapped in blankets as they gathered to watch the baggattaway game beginning outside the main entrance to the fort. This game is similar in form to lacrosse or field hockey. With an unlimited amount of players, each team used sticks with

ILLINOIS PRAIRIE DISTRICT LIBRARY

netted ends to lift and throw a ball towards the goal of the oppos-
ing team. The games were usually wildly aggressive with players
injured or even killed on occasion. The British soldiers, lulled by
the declaration of peace, came outside of the fort to watch the
game. The gates were wide open, the atmosphere relaxed.

When the ball was thrown over the wall, the soldiers retrieved
it so the game could continue. Soon the exuberant action caused
the ball to fly over the walls a second time. This time, the Native
Americans entered the fort. As they did, the women threw off their
blankets, revealing weapons that had been hidden underneath.
Completely taken by surprise, the British were overcome. Most
were massacred. A few of the higher-ranking officers and Ezekiel
Solomon were taken captive for purposes of negotiation.

While the French did not participate in the slaughter, neither
did they lift a hand to stop it. A few French did begrudgingly hide
individuals for a while. Alexander Henry found such a spot in a
neighbor's attic. He was discovered after a fearful night spent an-
ticipating the worst. Just when it looked hopeless for Henry, his
blood brother, Chief Wawatam claimed him as his prize on
grounds of Henry's adoption into the Chief's family. The Chief and
his family, with Henry, immediately left the fort. The kegs of whis-
key had been found and opened. The celebrating was becoming
dangerous for anyone who might happen to get in the way.

They headed to the safety of Mackinac Island. Here, Chief
Wawatam secreted an exhausted Alexander Henry into a cave.
Grateful, Henry wrapped a blanket around him and fell fast asleep.
The morning light revealed that he had spent the night on a pile of
human bones. As a traditional burial ground, Chief Wawatam had
deemed it the safest place for his new brother to hide. Today, Skull
Cave is roped off to discourage the curious. The bones have long
since disappeared.

The Native Americans maintained control of the fort for over
a year. Alexander Henry spent that year with his rescuers in a state

of capture. When he finally saw his chance, he made his escape and returned to trading at Fort Michilimackinac.

BECOMING AMERICAN

A new Treaty of Paris was signed 20 years later, in 1783. This time, the British were agreeing to the independence of their former North American colonies and ending the American Revolution. Michigan territory was given to the Americans and British rule officially ended. This does not mean that the British actually left. That took another thirteen years. The Americans were not strong enough to force the British out of the area after the protracted war they had just been through. So, the British continued on in their trading activities at Michilimackinac unhindered. Finally, the famous American war hero "Mad" Anthony Wayne set out to capture the western lands from the British. His prowess caused the British major in charge of Fort Michilimackinac to make a drastic decision. He relocated the fort to Mackinac Island. After dismantling the fort and salvaging all the materials he could, Major Patrick Sinclair ordered the burning of the old fort. Fort Mackinac, on Mackinac Island, was established in 1790. A lumber mill had been built on a creek east of the old fort. New lumber from Mill Creek was used to build a new and better settlement on the island. General Wayne never attacked the new fort.   His success in other parts of the frontier brought forth the Jay Treaty of 1794. At last, the United States had the right to occupy her lands.

A NEW CENTURY

John Jacob Astor established the American Fur Company in 1808. Millions of dollars worth of fur flowed through his headquarters on Mackinac Island, making Astor one of the richest men in America. Under his guidance, the American fur trade reached its zenith.

A brief skirmish with the British had resulted in British reoccupation of the island during the War of 1812. They built another fort, Fort George, on the high ground behind Fort Mackinac. The

Treaty of Ghent in 1815, once again, sent the British packing. John Astor and his fur company flourished throughout the fray. He would export beaver for thirty years. Mackinac Island became a boomtown as free enterprise opened up the area.

Missionaries came as well. The year 1825 welcomed the opening of the Mission House as a boarding school for Native American children. This was the first non-Catholic outreach. Located at Mission Point, it was founded by William and Amanda Ferry. They quickly added the Mission Church in 1829. It still stands and is the oldest church in the state. While here, their son, Thomas W. Ferry was born. He would one day become a United States senator. By the time Michigan became a state in 1837, the Ferrys realized that their mission on the island was no longer a vital component and abandoned their work for a new mission field.

The 1836 Treaty of Washington completed a settlement with the Native Americans of Michigan. In return for all of the land that surrounded the Straits of Mackinac and much more, they would receive yearly allotments and reservation areas. The Indian Dormitory, situated below Fort Mackinac, was built following this treaty. It was to serve as a school and distribution point for the tribes to receive their allotments.

The 1830s saw the virtual end of the fur trade. It would limp on for another decade in other places but never to the prosperity level that had been experienced at Mackinac Island. The American beaver was becoming extinct.

By 1849, Mackinac Island was experiencing an influx of travelers. Immigrants passed through the area to the copper and iron mines in the north, the rich farm lands of the west or even the gold mines of California. Mackinac Island was in the center of it all as people met and exchanged ideas, possibilities and new lives for old.

MACKINAW CITY

Time had seemed to stand still just across the waters at what was left of Michilimackinac. Edgar Conkling was a man with a vision as he laid plans for the somber shores. He was the first to name it Mackinaw City. He selected the English spelling of the name to differentiate his dream from the rest of the area. He envisioned a large city with boulevards and huge parks. In 1853, Mr. Conkling purchased the entire region of the northern Lower Peninsula from the United States Government. Surveying was completed in 1857. Blocks, lots and streets were all in place. The only thing missing was inhabitants.

THE DREAM COMES ALIVE

For close to a quarter of a century, Mr. Edgar Conkling carried the torch of hope for a thriving Mackinaw City. With this in mind, he built a dock in 1870. The workers who boarded in a shanty at the end of the dock were the first to reside in this yet unborn city. The purpose of the dock was to hold fuel wood for the steamer boats that plied the Great Lakes. This same year finally welcomed the first permanent citizens. Mr. And Mrs. George Stimpson purchased four lots from Mr. Conkling. They built a log cabin in the center of the lots on Central Avenue. Mackinaw City had its first home. Sailors and ship passengers alike began to descend on the Stimpson home in hopes of food and shelter. The Stimpsons responded with generous hospitality. Soon they constructed a larger building to accommodate all of the demands made upon them. The house was known as the Stimpson House well after the Stimpsons had sold it. That same year, Mr. And Mrs. L.I. Willetts arrived. They erected the first storefront in Mackinaw City. It was not yet the large metropolis that Edgar Conkling had envisioned, but Mackinaw City was making a start.

PAUL BUNYAN COMES TO MACKINAW CITY

The logging industry was now rising as the new star of Michigan commerce. Demand for logs from the prairie frontier and around the United States was reaching a crescendo. The woodless prairies were outgrowing their sod homes. Wood was needed to build the towns and homes of the newly prospering farmers. If Michigan had anything, it had wood. Enough lumber to build ten million six-bedroom homes was harvested from the standing pine timber between 1840 and 1900. Combined with the hardwood harvest of that same time frame, Michigan lumber production was such that the entire state and the state of Rhode Island could have been covered with a wood floor that was one inch thick.

Mackinaw City found itself in the center of this "green gold" rush. It was a natural site to gather the wood that would be shipped throughout the Great Lakes. More docks were added and, finally, the railroad reached the tip of the Lower Peninsula. The first train to arrive in Mackinaw City whistled in just a few days after the death of Mackinaw's visionary, Edgar Conkling. He passed away in December of 1881 while overseeing work on Mackinaw City, Illinois. Conkling Heritage Park on Mackinaw's waterfront commemorates this amazing man.

The village had grown enough that they established the first town school in 1883. It was an exciting, thriving time. Burly loggers with their tall tales of Paul Bunyan and his blue ox, Babe, shared the dining tables with polished businessmen from the east. People from places like New York, Detroit and Chicago arrived seeking the clean, fresh air. Mackinaw City and Mackinac Island were recommended as a treatment for respiratory distresses including allergies and asthma. Overshadowed by the chant of the loggers' stories, a new industry was taking a foothold. This would prove to be the most enduring of them all.

By 1900, most of the white pine forests in Michigan had been decimated. Between overzealous logging and several massive wild fires, the lumber industry was forced to reinvent itself. It did this with the help of furniture makers in places south of Mackinaw City. As the logging industry quietly left center stage, the tourism and resort industry of Michigan stepped into the limelight.

Did you know... ?

Although cars are banned on Mackinac Island, emergency vehicles and (in winter) snowmobiles are exempt from this rule.

The Mackinac Bridge

The Mackinac Bridge is a suspension bridge with a total length of about five miles. The two towers stand 3,800 feet apart, and at a dizzying height of 552 feet above the water. The steel in each of these towers weighs an impressive 6,500 tons. Added to the rest of the components, the bridge tips the scale at 1,024,500 tons. Superb engineering planned for the effects of weather with a deck that can move right or left as much as 35 feet at the center span. Colored lights line the cables to create an outline of the bridge during the night.

Governor G. Mennen Williams declared the bridge "another Northwest Passage" during his speech at the dedication of the Mackinac Bridge on November 1, 1957. The project had commenced a mere three years earlier. The Mackinac Bridge has been designated by the Michigan Section of the *American Society of Engineers* as the number one civil engineering project for Michigan in the 20th century. It is the third longest suspension bridge in the world, with its distance of 8,614 feet between cable anchorages. It is longer than the renowned Golden Gate Bridge of San Francisco Bay. Affectionately nicknamed the "Mighty Mac," the bridge's design took aesthetics into consideration right from the outset. The intent was to not only produce an effective link for the state, but a memorial to the fortitude of every person that has poured themselves into the making of the past, present and future of Michigan.

BEFORE THE BRIDGE

The very first person to make the strenuous paddle across the waters of the Straits of Mackinac probably wished for a better way. It is a treacherous stretch of water. One minute it will be as calm as a sleeping baby and the next as wild as a tiger. As transportation evolved, the gap between peninsulas posed a growing inconvenience. Growth in industry and population brought the need to join

the two peninsulas into the forefront. Various plans for a bridge
had been drawn and proposed since the mid-1800s. Realistically,
the technology needed was not available at that time. It was a
common joke that the upper and lower peninsulas of Michigan
were only engaged, but not quite married.

Car ferries were active in the early 1900s to fill the transportation needs of travelers and commerce. The State of Michigan established ferry service in 1923 to meet the rush of new tourists travel-
ling by a newer mode of transportation – the automobile. Mackinaw City quickly added motels and other facilities to accommodate
this influx of travelers. Some local residents still tell stories of the
hours spent waiting in line to use the ferries. The hospitable people
often made an outing of the wait. Picnic baskets adorned the tail-
gates and running boards of vehicles up and down the line. However, on a day-to-day basis, the wait was tedious and slowed down
the activities of a burgeoning economy.

PRENTISS M. BROWN

Attorney Prentiss M. Brown was born in St. Ignace in 1889. An up-
and-coming lawyer, he and his partner had been diligently prepar-
ing to argue a case before the Michigan Supreme Court. To reach
Lansing, they would have to cross the Straits of Mackinac and take
a train from Mackinaw City to the capitol during a harsh winter.
The ferries were immobilized by ice and a storm was brewing. They
engaged the aid of a horse and cutter and headed out. Hummocks
forced them to repeatedly alter their course. These ice hills grew
larger and more frequent the farther they traveled. Winds hurled
sleet and ice crystals at the travelers. The snow was sharp and
blinding as they scurried towards the southern shore. They eventually arrived in Mackinaw City across miles of ice, through gale-force
winds and snow only to find that they had missed their train. This
event seared the conscience of Prentiss Brown with the absolute
necessity of finding a better way to cross the straits.

Following a childhood spent enjoying the best of the North Country, Brown worked as a bellhop on Mackinac Island. From this humble position, he completed his law training and passed the Michigan bar exam. His legal career was short-lived, however. From 1932 until 1943, he served his fellow citizens in the U.S. Congress and Senate in Washington, D.C. In spite of his many successes, his most rewarding accomplishment was his appointment in 1950 to the Mackinac Bridge Authority. During his tenure as leader of this group, financing for the Mackinac Bridge was secured.

Prentiss' childhood had been filled with talk of a bridge and many other schemes to join the two peninsulas. Some plans were wild, calling for "floating tunnels" or a series of bridges linking all of the islands to the peninsulas. Most were straightforward; just build a bridge from St. Ignace to Mackinaw City. Past committees had investigated the probability and the costs, particularly after bridges in New York and San Francisco were completed. A state-appointed Bridge Authority had researched and made a reasonable proposal in 1928. The economics of that time forced the shelving of the bridge project and that group was dissolved. The committee formed in 1950 was an aggressive, determined group. With Prentiss Brown leading the way, they demolished obstacles and found financing for their dream. Today, Prentiss is considered the "Father of the Mackinac Bridge."

CONNECTING MICHIGAN

Official ceremonies held in May of 1954, in both St. Ignace and Mackinaw City, marked the commencement of work on the bridge. Designed by engineer Dr. David Steinman, the bridge would require the largest bridge construction fleet ever assembled up to that time. Five workers died during the construction, giving their lives for this long-cherished dream. Soberly the work of creating a link between Michigan's upper and lower peninsulas was completed.

June 25, 1998 witnessed bridge's 100 millionth crossing. It occurred 40 years after the opening of the "Mighty Mac" in 1958.

The bridge has not only physically linked the upper and lower peninsulas; it has united the residents of Michigan together in intangible ways. For many families, a visit to the Mackinac Bridge has become a favorite tradition. It evokes a sense of peace and relaxation while promising excitement and endless adventure. After more than fifty years, "Mighty Mac" is like an old friend welcoming those who gather at the straits.

Did you know... ?

*John Jacob Astor started the **American Fur Company** in 1808. The **American Fur Company Store** on Mackinac Island still exists today.*

Area Orientation

A visit to Mackinac is a tradition for many families. Not just from Michigan, visitors come to Mackinac from Chicago, Ohio, Canada and beyond the Great Lakes region. But why should Mackinac be the destination of choice? The answer is as varied as those who attempt to define Mackinac. Shopkeepers boast about the unique shopping. Those in the hospitality industry point to their superb service.

The quick answer, however, is location. Mackinaw City and Mackinac Island give the grandest view of two truly Great Lakes at one moment. Visitors can watch the sunset while the moon rises. Standing on the shores of the Great Lakes offers a very different experience than from being by the ocean.

From Mackinaw City, visitors can spend their days exploring the wilderness on carefully mapped trails, or stepping back in time through museums and historical displays located on the actual sites. Mackinac Island affords easy transition from the finest of urban conveniences to the spiraling rock formations of nature and the ease of country life. Day trips in all directions provide individualized adventure. A nightly return to the city or island keeps vacation time available for its true purpose and eliminates the hassle of continual packing and re-establishing.

MACKINAC OR MACKINAW?

The turtle-shaped island today called Mackinac and the surrounding area has had its share of inhabitants, and its share of names. From the earliest names "michinimakinagog" and "michinimikana" to the more modern "michilimackinac" and "mackinac," the name has changed with the times. It is thought that the original name means simply "turtle," describing the shape of the island, but this is not known for sure.

The Algonquin word "michinimikana" makes its own claim as the original name for the area. To the French, the word sounded like "michilimackinac." Common use eventually shortened it to "mackinac." The final sound of the word is pronounced as an "aw." The British were never great favorites of the earliest inhabitants, so their version remained fairly obscure until Mackinaw City was platted in 1853. This spelling was deliberately selected in order to differentiate the city from the rest of the area.

Regardless of the spelling, it is pronounced "mack-in-aw." The French spelling of "mackinac" refers to the entire area – the island, straits, bridge and so forth. "Mackinaw" is only applied to the city on the Lower Peninsula. "Michilimackinac" is still used today by the state park system to reference the restored fort on the mainland.

THE STRAITS OF MACKINAC

Michigan and the Great Lakes were formed at the end of the last major ice age. A warming climate stalled the colossal movements of the glaciers. Melting ice covered the area with vast amounts of water. This was a slow process, covering large quantities of time. The retreating glaciers left valleys, hills and giant hollows in their wake.

A "strait" is any narrow channel that joins two large bodies of water. The Great Lakes are connected to each other by a series of straits, rivers, and smaller bodies of water, including the Straits of Mackinac, the Niagara River, the St. Clair and Detroit Rivers (via Lake St. Clair), and the St. Marys River. Using the man-made Erie Canal, ships could travel from Duluth, Minnesota or Chicago, Illinois (and many points in between) all the way to the Atlantic Ocean.

These waterway connections have served many uses. During the 1800s, the Upper Peninsula shipped hundreds of Christmas trees to urban destinations on the shores of Lake Michigan. Known as the "Christmas Tree Ships," the sailors would string lights on the ships to add to the festive nature of their cargo. For places like Chicago, this signaled the beginning of the holiday.

The Straits of Mackinac – with the plural "straits" to encompass the multiple straits in the surrounding waterways – spans five miles from shore to shore. The unique depths required the foundational piers of the Mackinac Bridge to be established at 210 feet deep – it is more common for straits to be fairly shallow. Many are home to one or more rapids and waterfalls. The power of the glaciers slowly gouged the straits while immense amounts of water were deposited.

UPPER AND LOWER PENINSULAS

Michigan is made up of two large peninsulas. The southern, or *Lower Peninsula,* is roughly shaped as a mitten, the thumb on the right side. Michigan residents can describe their location within the state simply by displaying their hand. The *Upper Peninsula* covers an expanse north of Wisconsin, Michigan, and Lake Michigan, and is bordered on the north by Lake Superior.

Mackinaw City stands at the northern most point of the Lower Peninsula. It is the epitome of the phrase "up north." The term "downstate" is defined by how close one resides to this point. For the most part, anything south of an imaginary line running from west to east through Cadillac, Michigan is "downstate." "Yoopers" (as in "Upper Peninsula"-ers, or "U.P."-ers) refers to the hardy residents of the Upper Peninsula. "Islanders" naturally addresses the residents of Mackinac Island and the surrounding islands.

VISITING MACKINAC

Another unchanging factor of Mackinaw City and Mackinac Island is the cross section of people who are drawn to the area. First and foremost are the families. They come for fun and as a tradition.

Couples, young and old, visit for the romance and adventure. Lives have been pledged to each other during Labor Day walks across the Mackinac Bridge, on fort walls and along the shores at twilight. Nature lovers come in groups and alone to search out the delicate forest flora and to track the secretive birds of the northern Midwest.

Divers charter boats and investigate the mystery of shipwrecks deep beneath the waves. Bicyclists arrive with scheduled tours during three seasons of the year. Individual bicyclists enjoy the challenge packed into visits to the island. Snowmobilers converge on this point closest to the Upper Peninsula of Michigan.

At any given moment during the warm seasons, people from all across the globe can be found enjoying themselves here. Mackinac Island has hosted those who prefer leather clothing and purple striped hair while also hosting a family of country farmers. Smiles lit up their faces as they enjoyed the shared carriage ride. The ancient nickname of "The Gathering Place" still applies.

WHAT TO DO

Outdoor activities make up much of the area's offerings. Water adventures in particular play a part of every vacation to Mackinaw City and Mackinac Island. Swimming in the waterparks and in pools is a getaway highlight for many who come. Hiking, fishing, boating and snowmobiling are favorites. Sightseeing fills time for both visitors and locals. Mackinaw City and Mackinac Island are great places to indulge in shopping. Festivals and shows fill the calendar in both places. These celebrations honor historic events, natural wonders and some are just for fun. Shows run the gamut from antiques to cars to re-enactments.

Private group events bring many visitors to Mackinaw City and Mackinac Island. Reunions, conventions and retreats fill the hospitality schedules. The natural beauty and the exquisite gardens found throughout the area offer backdrops for weddings. It is a delight to stroll the island on any summer weekend and observe the carriages transporting fairytale wedding parties. Events in the city can be elegant or whimsical. Wedding parties enjoying a hayride to their reception have been seen around town. Opportunities abound for things to do.

WHAT TO BRING

Assuming the basics are covered, some additional items specific to a vacation in Mackinac are suggested. For starters, even at the height of the summer heat, a sweater or light jacket is useful. Breezes from off of the water can be quite cool, especially on a ferry speeding across the straits. A pair of comfortable walking shoes is the most important "must pack" item. Mackinaw City and Mackinac Island are all about walking.

If any hiking is planned, long pants and shoes with socks are the best outfit. Even in hot weather, they offer prime protection against insects and poison ivy. There are too many lovely things to see in the woods to spend energy wondering about poison ivy and ticks. All woods have them and it is just better not to take them home. Insect repellent would be a nice addition, but is not necessary. The constant breeze keeps the straits area relatively (but not completely) free of mosquitoes and their buddies.

Unless formal attire is needed for a special event or the dinner hour at the Grand Hotel, it is best left home. Souvenirs will quickly fill that empty spot in the travel case. Lastly, a restatement of the obvious seems necessary: bring the camera and video equipment along with the necessary chargers. Phone charger, too!

GETTING TO MACKINAC

The trip to Mackinaw City and then to Mackinac Island is part of the fun. A host of routes and methods of transportation add an aura of adventure right from the beginning. Unless you are piloting a private airplane to Mackinac Island, at least two different methods of transportation will be necessary. Every trip to the area can be made with a fresh approach or with the relaxing influence of the tried and true favorite path.

ARRIVING BY LAND

If you are headed north in Michigan's Lower Peninsula, all roads eventually lead to Mackinaw City. Interstate 75 (I-75) connects directly to the Mackinac Bridge. From Detroit, simply follow I-75 north. Northbound exits 337, 338 and 339 access Mackinaw City. Exit 337 opens to the south side of downtown. This hosts the largest selection of hotels and two ferry docks to Mackinac Island. Shoreline campgrounds are also in this part of town. Exit 338 takes you into town with a more direct route. Here is the main shopping strip with some hotels and is the hub of it all. One ferry dock is located in this area as is the Mackinaw City Municipal Marina. The final exit before the bridge, Exit 339, offers the easiest approach to Colonial Michilimackinac with shoreline day parks for picnicking and views of the residential areas.

To arrive from the western side of the state from places such as Chicago and Grand Rapids, there are several options. One of the nicest drives is along Lake Michigan via U.S. 31. This route is scenic and relaxing. In May and early June, cherry trees blossom as you approach the Grand Traverse Bay portion of the journey. The sheer volume of trees in blossom is a magnificent sight. It can have some long isolated stretches between towns. It is the road "less traveled" so traffic is not much of a hassle. U.S. 131 out of Grand Rapids is direct and quick. U.S. 131 joins U.S. 31 in Petoskey, Michigan. Stay north and U.S. 31 combines with I-75 just south of Mackinaw City. I-96 from Chicago has exits for both of these options.

Mid-Michigan routes from the Lansing area are straightforward. Follow U.S. 27 or U.S. 131 north until they merge with I-75. U.S. 131 swings west to Grand Rapids. U.S. 27 heads north and is the more direct course. Mid-Michigan is farm country. The orderly fields spread out on Michigan's plains are dotted with picturesque farms and small woods. Wild deer love this area and are usually seen early morning or late afternoon into evening. They do not obey traffic laws, of course, so keep a sharp watch for those crossing the road.

Michigan winters are hard on the road surfaces. Summer construction is a certain thing. Be sure to check your chosen route for any delays that may occur. Even with construction, the traffic usually moves along fairly well. Avoiding the population dense areas during rush hours may help facilitate your drive.

BY BUS OR TRAIN

At this time, passenger trains do not reach northern Michigan. There is an agreement between **Amtrak** *(⟨ amtrak.com)* and **Greyhound** *(⟨ greyhound.com)* to bring passengers from the northernmost Amtrak stations via the Greyhound bus line route to St. Ignace. From that point, transportation to the Island and to Mackinaw City must be arranged independently. This itinerary adds quite a bit of time to the journey and is a less direct path to the destinations desired.

This is not the most convenient route but it is better than missing out on a visit. Many groups charter independent bus lines to make the trip. A check with local clubs and travel agents can alert travelers to any pending trips. These chartered rides are very popular and can be tailored to special interests or needs.

MACKINAC BRIDGE TOLLS

There is a toll of $3.00 per car or $1.50 per axle to cross the Mackinac Bridge. All other vehicles pass for a toll of $3.50 per axle. The monies obtained are used to maintain and update the bridge. The Mackinac Bridge does not connect Mackinac Island with the mainland; it only connects the two peninsulas.

AIR TRAVEL

Arriving by air offers the best perspective of the area. There is simply no other way that showcases the landscape as well. Inland lakes that are hidden from view at ground level sparkle like hidden treasure from the air. Autumn colors are always beautiful, but viewed from above they are breathtaking. The unique geography of the straits is best understood from a bird's eye view. Even for non-geography buffs, this is a sight worth seeing.

Local area airports enjoy their unique positions and their excitement shows in many helpful ways. They are home to personable flight enthusiasts. The local aviation club is a showcase of vintage aircraft and intricate hand crafted flying machines. You never know who or what will be flying in. It is a wonderful, non-traditional way to view the Mackinac Bridge, island and surrounding area.

PELLSTON REGIONAL AIRPORT

(Airport Code: PLN ☎ *231.539.8441* ✈ *pellstonairport.com)* The Pellston Regional Airport, just south of Mackinaw City, is the largest airport in the area. Its rustic log cabin style décor is home to the only major airline carrier that reaches the tip of the Lower Peninsula. It is well organized and easily accommodates larger planes. It is situated on U.S. 31. Transportation from the airport will need to be arranged. The drive takes about twenty minutes. Some of the hotels offer shuttle service, as do some private companies. The airport personnel can be reached to assist in making these arrangements. Car rentals and taxi service are also available.

MACKINAC COUNTY AIRPORT

(☎ *906.643.7327, code 83D)* The Mackinac County Airport is equipped with hangars and tiedowns. The 3,800 foot concrete runway and surrounding buildings are kept in good condition. Unicom 122.7 is the activation code. **Great Lakes Air** *(*☎

906.643.7165) at Mackinac County Airport offers charter flights to and from Mackinac Island for reasonable rates. These pilots are thoroughly qualified and fly in almost any weather. They make the short flight to Mackinac Island into a treat and really should be experienced if possible.

MACKINAC ISLAND AIRPORT

(☎ 906.847.3231, code MCD) Run by the Mackinac Island State Park Commission, the Mackinac Island Airport features a 3,500-foot asphalt runway. They meticulously maintain the landing strip and supporting equipment. All hotels and resorts on Mackinac Island provide shuttle service to/from the airport (by horse-drawn carriages or snowmobiles, depending on the season). All flights to the island use this airport.

MACKINAC ISLAND BY WATER

Arriving by water is the favored connection to Mackinac Island. While modern boats have replaced the voyageurs' canoes, the travel time of 15-20 minutes (depending on waves and weather) to the island from Mackinaw City is about the same. For all of our technology, the expertise and muscle of the original natives and voyageurs cannot be bested.

Three ferry lines offer service to and from Mackinac Island with departure points in both St. Ignace and Mackinaw City. Seating ranges from benches on the open-air top decks to booth or theater style fold down seats in the enclosed lower decks. Huge windows frame excellent views of the straits. Please bring a sweater or jacket for the ride across, even in the summertime. The ferry offices on Mackinac Island have rental lockers available for a nominal fee. They are large enough to stash jackets and a few other things that you may not want to carry around the island with you. The Mackinaw City docks are larger and accommodate a higher customer volume. Each of the lines offers free shuttle service to and from the local hotels and campgrounds. Handicap services and luggage service are standard features. While all three have their service perfected, they each have their own unique signature to put on the trip across the straits.

Ticket prices between the ferry companies are comparable as is the travel time to and from the island. Personal preference is the only real factor in picking a ferry line. All offer the highest safety considerations and excellent service. Ferry service from St. Ignace is also available, for those that are arriving from the north.

SHEPLER'S

(☎ *800.828.6157* ✆ *sheplersferry.com*) Shepler's Mackinac Island Ferry hosts the **Gateway to Mackinac Island**, a grand arch entrance to their facility. It is the most visible of the ferry lines from downtown. Shepler's has an elegant feel to their service. They depart the Mackinaw City docks May through October with daily trips that vary in scheduled frequency ranging every hour or half hour, depending on customer volume. They depart with similar schedules from the St. Ignace docks for April through November. Schedules are available at businesses throughout town and online.

STAR LINE

(☎ *800.638.9892* ✆ *mackinacferry.com*) Star Line Mackinac Island Ferry is the smallest of the ferry lines and offers a friendly, down home atmosphere. The genuine smiles and friendly attention of their team puts even the most nervous traveler at ease. They feature the famous "rooster tail" water spray behind their hydro-jet ferries. If you are riding on the top deck of one of these ferries, expect some water spray. Not drenching, just enough to make it feel like a "walk on the wild side." It is fun and the kids will love it. Daily runs from Mackinaw City are scheduled on the hour or half hour, May to through October. Runs from St. Ignace are made beginning in April and ending in November. Updated schedules are available everywhere in town or online.

ARNOLD LINE

(☎ *800.542.8528* ✆ *arnoldline.com)* Arnold Transit Company uses catamarans with twin hull structures to cruise to the island. This makes for the smoothest ride across the straits. They also have the largest carrying capacity per boat. Like the other lines, Arnold offers daily trips on the hour or half hour departing Mackinaw City from May through October and from St. Ignace for April through November.

MARINAS

For those with their own watercraft, the area has several locations to dock and service private boats.

MACKINAW CITY MUNICIPAL MARINA

(☎ *231.436.5269 for harbormaster's line during the summer season/ 231.436.5351 for during off season/800.44.PARKS for reservations)* The Mackinaw City Municipal Marina is located east of the Mackinac Bridge and Colonial Michilimackinac. This is a relatively quiet marina, with a lovely park and historic walkway separating it from the businesses of downtown. It offers 26 seasonal and 78 transient dockage sites with all of the amenities expected from a quality dock, including grocery delivery service, laundry, showers and more. The marina monitors channels 9 and 16 on marine radio.

MACKINAC ISLAND STATE DOCK

(☎ *906.847.3561 for harbormaster/800.44.PARKS for reservations)* For those with their own watercraft, mooring at Mackinac Island State Dock is offered through the Michigan Department of Natural Resources. This is a busy marina. Not only are the ferries constantly coming and going, the slips are located directly behind some of the island's finest eateries and saloons. It has an ambiance all of its own due to the clip-clop of the horses, the shouts of the dock workers and the overall hustle and bustle. Just by sitting casually on your boat, you join in the excitement of downtown Mackinac Island. They offer 63 transient slips and 13 seasonal slips. The transient slips have a four-day maximum time limit. The amenities at this site meet the standard expectations, including hookups, picnic areas, restrooms, showers and boat maintenance facilities. Marine radio channel 9 is monitored by the island marina. Reservations are highly recommended but not required.

GETTING AROUND MACKINAW CITY

Harried drivers and traffic jams find no place in northern Michigan. Driving your own vehicle in Mackinaw City and the surrounding area offers the most flexibility. The city's founder, Edgar Conkling, included wide, tree-lined boulevards in his city plans back in the 1850s. That foresight has given the city plenty of room for parking. Central Avenue features such a boulevard, divided for traffic flow.

The traffic plan allows for wonderful, easy parking down the center. There are spaces that readily fit motor homes, buses and cars with trailers. Some are marked specifically for compact cars. All are wide enough for easy in and out access. There are no meters to pay, so the entire day can be spent enjoying Mackinaw City instead of worrying about parking.

EXPLORING ON FOOT

Walking is serious business in Mackinaw City. Bring comfortable shoes and plan on covering quite a bit of ground. This is the best and easiest way to get around the main portions of Mackinaw City. The village is so committed to hospitality that in 2000 they completed a new sidewalk project that paved their walkways with red brick. The sidewalks were also widened to better accommodate strollers, wheelchairs and other walking aids. Skateboarding and rollerblading are forbidden on the sidewalks out of consideration for the majority of visitors.

Brick planters surround trees and flowers. Many people sit and "people watch" from these vantage points while eating ice cream. After almost a decade of wear, the sidewalks have only faded a bit in color. They extend past the main shopping area to include a scenic walk along the shore and out to Colonial Michilimackinac. Historic markers dot this red brick route giving interesting information. A stroll down this part of the sidewalk is a favorite way to wind down at the end of a busy day.

SHUTTLES
Many of the local hotels and campgrounds offer shuttle service to and from the ferry dock of your choice. Those that are out of easy walking range of the downtown area also offer service by request to and from town. Shuttle service is available to the national parks. There may be a slight charge for this service. Otherwise, these services are complimentary and may be arranged as necessary through your host facility.

WINTER TRANSPORTATION
Winter brings snow and ice. For year-round residents of Mackinac Island, this means a dangerous trek for the horses. Snowmobiling is allowed on the island during the snowy months. The horses are safely stabled and residents use snowmobiles instead. Visitors are welcome to join the fun by riding their sleds across the ice bridge from St. Ignace to the island. This bridge is formed when the water between the Upper Peninsula and the island freezes over. It is lined with old Christmas trees to mark the approved route.

Mackinac Island Transportation

Except for emergency vehicles, cars are prohibited on Mackinac Island. This rare trait is one of Mackinac Island's most cherished assets, and the story of how Mackinac Island became a hold out against the mechanization of transportation is worth the telling. This is one instance where the political maneuvers created something far grander than was initially imagined.

HORSE AND CARRIAGE

Carriage tours of the island began as soon as there were folks willing to pay for the service. Officially, the industry began with the issuing of the first carriage license in 1869. These independent carriage drivers vied for patrons even as the prospective customers docked. As many as 80 carriages gathered at the docks, blocking the streets. Competition was fierce and, at times, a bit unfriendly. There was enough business to go around, so nothing truly detrimental is recorded as having happened. Then, one bright day, a sports fisherman arrived at the docks with a shiny new automobile. He quickly cranked it up and hit the streets of Mackinac Island, honking at the slower moving carriages in his way. His vehicle sputtered smoke and fumes into the air. He frightened patrons, horses, drivers and everyone else near him. With a wave and a smile to the chaos his entrance had created, he set off for his favorite fishing spot.

The carriage drivers found the situation untenable. It was one thing to compete among themselves, but to share the roadways with such a nuisance? They had heard stories of these menaces. Once one of these contraptions arrived, others were sure to follow. This posed some immediate concerns. The chief concern was that patronage of the carriages would diminish if people began to bring their own transportation to the island. Safety concerns nestled right up near the top as additional horseless carriages arrived. Injuries were being reported daily as a result of the noise and careless use of these vehicles. People and horses were subjected to horrific accidents. Eventually, death resulted. There was no other option but to act against these monstrosities if the peace and welfare of the island was to be preserved. Of course, preserving the carriage tour livelihood would also be a welcome result.

The carriage men formed an association. This association monitored fair business practices, care of the animals and other necessities that brought the industry to higher standards. (Today, the practices of the Mackinac Island Carriage Association set the world standard.) Now that they had addressed their own difficulties, the carriage men, led by Thomas Chambers, petitioned the Village of Mackinac Island to ban the horseless carriages. Their association gave them newfound political power. Using a paper full of signatures, they won their battle against the foul mechanized transportation. The year 1896 marked the end of the invasion.

Islanders waited anxiously to see how visitors would react to the ban. Their very own State of Michigan had begun the American love affair with the automobile. With this act, one of Michigan's most cherished communities was thumbing its nose at its own promising industrial romance. While the rest of the state and nation hurried pell-mell into the motorized future, Mackinac Island said a quiet "no" and then held her breath.

A strange thing happened as the first island guests arrived after the ban. Yes, some were disgruntled at having to leave their new toy behind. For the most part, travelers turned off the motors and headed for the relief of life, as they had known it. Nostalgia for the quieter, simpler time of the recent past was already beginning. Oddly, this detestable machine (or, rather, the lack of it) brought more visitors than ever before to the shores of Mackinac Island. The petition had not only saved the carriage industry but had prospered it. The unique ambiance of Mackinac Island was born.

Descendants of these original carriage men continue to wield political power on the island in order to preserve this precious heritage. They proudly point to the six generations of expertise that it has taken to build the specialized herd of horses used on Mackinac Island. Each winter the herd is ferried to the Upper Peninsula. Here they consume 900 tons of hay, 4,000 bushels of grain and 120 tons of Master Mix. This mix is a special feed developed for horses in severe winter climates by Dr. Bill Chambers. A resident of the island, Dr. Chambers is one of the many among the generations of carriage families that have developed improved tack and care methods for the horses. For them, carriage life on Mackinac Island is a matter of honor. They are protecting the largest carriage herd and finest carriage tradition in the world. In this day of rapid change, that is quite a respectable accomplishment.

The changing island population threatens this lifestyle as residents grow older and no longer maintain their own stables. New residents of the island often lack the expertise, desire and/or finances necessary to stable their own horses. This presents the problem of islanders having to rely on bicycling, walking or renting a taxi. In a world built on instant gratification, the island's slower pace can be frustrating. Through the years, compromises have been made to address these issues. Emergency vehicles are completely modern, enabling swift response to crisis. Snowmobiles are allowed in the winter to expedite movement around the island and across the straits. This relieves the enormous isolation once endured by year-round inhabitants.

BICYCLES, BUILT FOR ONE OR TWO

About the same time that horseless carriages were banned on Mackinac Island, another wonderful invention was coming into its own. By 1899, America was producing one million bicycles a year. Within a decade, the infatuation gave way to the drama of the motorcar and the motorcycle. This loss of enthusiasm affected most of the nation. For Mackinac Island, the bicycle was a welcome alternative to the growing expense of owning horses. The younger set of island inhabitants especially enjoyed the independence and

speed the invention brought them. Everyone else may let their bicycles gather dust, but not here. Even today, watching islanders on
their bicycles is fascinating. They have developed the ride into a
fine art of balance and precision timing. It is common to see bikers
load enormous baskets, attached to the handlebars, and smoothly
peddle off. Two-wheeled bicycle carts attach to the back of their
bikes and haul everything from groceries to children and the family
dog. For those more accustomed to thinking of bicycles in terms of
exercise and racing, this basic use is mesmerizing.

Bicycling on Mackinac Island offers a refreshing chance to
really enjoy oneself. Without the presence of motor vehicles, the
open road beckons. Young and old are welcome to experience the
independence of biking where they want to go, when they want to
get there and at what pace. There are no designated "bike trails" on
the island. They are all considered to be roads and are equally
shared with horses and pedestrians. The majority of roads are
paved. Getting lost is not an option. All roads lead eventually to the
shoreline. Follow the paved, carless highway and one is guaranteed
to arrive downtown. Bicycling here is not about speed, technique
or any of those kinds of pressures. It is about letting kids of all ages
spread their proverbial wings and flying. One word of caution, cy-
clists will be tempted to try the "Look, Ma, no hands!" trick. Practice it at your own risk.

Mackinac Island bicycle rentals also offer the choice of renting
a tandem bicycle. This "bicycle built for two" provides an adventurous and practical option. Sweethearts can strengthen their rela-
tionships, parents can boost a child's confidence; anything is possible on a bicycle built for two. Professionals utilize them in races
and endurance competitions. Thankfully, it does not take a professional to enjoy the experience of riding a tandem bike. With a few
helpful pieces of advice from those in the know, anyone can take a
spin with ease.

While it is tantalizing to mount a tandem bike as if one was a
heroic cowboy, this method should be avoided. Since the person

riding in the back usually is first in place, when the driver lets out a whoop and tosses a leg carelessly across the bike, the rider in back is in danger of a kick in the face. Ridiculous as it sounds, this sorry event has been witnessed several times. Another method that is repeated by novices is the idea of having the second rider mount and then the front rider grabs the handlebars and makes a running start before attempting to take their seat. This comical sight is welcome entertainment for on-lookers but is never successful for the riders.

The tried and true method, recommended by tandem riders the world over, is easy, even if it isn't glamorous. Beginning with the front rider holding the bicycle, both riders stand astride the bike with both feet on the ground. While the front rider maintains this position, the second rider slightly lifts the back of the bike in order to rotate the pedal towards the top. Without pushing the pedal, the rider then sits on the seat, feet in position. The front rider repeats these moves with the addition of the initial pedal push to keep from toppling over. Try to get up to speed as quickly as possible for a smoother ride. Count any false starts as practice and enjoy the accomplishment.

An entire terminology and technique has grown up around these legends from song. The front rider is called the "pilot" or "captain." This comes with two responsibilities: control the bike and communicate. The second rider is not a passenger but an equal participant in the venture. The captain should advise of any bumps, turns and so forth that the second rider may not see. The captain controls the vehicle through balance, steering, shifting and brakes. Knowing this division of responsibilities ahead of time really helps keep the peace. Referred to as the "stoker" or "rear admiral," the second rider provides power. This rider needs to warn the pilot of any weight shifting that may be needed due to saddle soreness or other reasons. An unpredictable weight shift can break the rhythm and throw the bike off of balance. Remember, back seat driving is unwelcome and usually not necessary. Instead, take the pictures, read the maps and lead the trail song.

There is a freedom in the transportation modes available on Mackinac Island. By being forced into a more natural pace, life takes on a new zest. There is a sense of pride that comes from biking around the island, whether on our own or with family and friends. No matter how often this is accomplished, that sense of satisfaction is not diminished. Carriage rides present a different perspective. Imagination comes alive, regardless of how long it has been dormant. Seated in a carriage, anyone can take a flight of fancy and become a pioneer, a wealthy socialite or an undercover agent on a secret mission. Transportation on Mackinac Island is an integral part of what Mackinac is all about.

GETTING AROUND MACKINAC ISLAND

Travel on Mackinac Island expressly excludes motor vehicles. Urged on by citizens in the late 1890s, the city council banned motor vehicles because they frightened the horses. That law remains in effect with allowances for modern emergency vehicles, electric wheelchairs and/or strollers.

HIGHWAY M-185
Michigan's shortest highway, M-185, circles the island. It is the only highway maintained by taxes on fuel for motor vehicles that does not allow use by those same vehicles. The irony of this suits the dry northern sense of humor well. Additional modern considerations forbid skateboards and roller blades in the downtown area and on M-185.

The road circles the entire island, which is less than 10 miles, and provides some of the best views of Mackinac and the straits. Bicycles are the vehicles of choice on M-185. The "highway" brings travelers through the Mackinac Island State Park and right into downtown Mackinac Island. A series of mileposts lead the way.

BICYCLE RENTALS

The ferry lines routinely charge a small fee to bring your own bicycle to the island. This is definitely the best way to go. It is cheaper than renting and you will be most comfortable on your own bike. Traveling with bikes and hauling them on and off of car bike racks may be a hassle for some visitors. Depending on what else needs to be handled, bringing bikes could be an unwanted complication.

As soon as you exit the dock areas, bicycle rental shops are waiting. This is probably the most popular way to navigate around the island on your own. Rentals may be arranged by the hour or day. Tag-alongs and baby seats are available options. The majority of the bikes offered are single speed. Bicycle selections include mountain bikes, children's bikes and tandems (bicycles built for two).

Close to a dozen companies offer rentals. The following companies offer all of the above and also offer options such as Electric Amigos, wheelchairs and adult strollers for those in need of the additional services: **Ryba's Bike Rental** (☎ *906.847.6261*), **Mackinac Island Bike Shop** (☎ *906.847.6337*), and **Orr-Kid's Bike Shop** (☎ *906.847.3211*), which offers repair services as well.

HORSE AND CARRIAGE

This is what traversing Mackinac Island is all about. From Percheron draft horses to exquisite Irish Hackney, the island is filled with beautiful horses. Dray carts pulled by the large draft horses carry equipment, groceries and other loads. The carriage horses seem delicate by comparison. Visitors may visit the Grand Hotel's stables for complimentary viewing or they may stop by the paddock at Surrey Hills to visit the draft horses.

Hotel and resort guests generally receive a complimentary horse-drawn carriage ride to their accommodations. Many of the bed and breakfast homes offer this as well. The Grand Hotel is particularly noted for its shining black carriages with attendants in full livery dress. The stable at the Grand Hotel is especially interesting with its museum of historical carriages and spotless tack displays.

Two companies bring the opportunity to explore by horseback or driving your own buggy. Both offer orientation for the uninitiated in horse maneuvering. This is a fine opportunity to try something new. **Cindy's Riding Stable** *(☎ 906.847.5372 ⏐ cindysridingstable.com)* specializes in saddle horses for riding the wooded trails outside of the downtown area. They provide maps, instruction and safety gear. They are a busy place so calling a head is a good idea. At **Jack's Livery Stable** *(☎ 906.847.3391 ⏐ jacksliverystable.com),* customers walk away smiling. The satisfaction of driving a horse and buggy on your own can't be hidden. Jack's gives thorough instruction before sending drivers out. This is a good option for families or groups.

MACKINAC ISLAND CARRIAGE TOURS [MUST SEE]

(☎ 906.847.3307 ⏐ mict.com) Mackinac Island Carriage Tours is the world's oldest and largest continually-operated horse and buggy livery. More than 400 horses convey passenger and freight carriages all over the island. Narrated tours take just under three hours and visit the key sites around the island. For over a century, these tours have been offered to island guests.

As the carriages leave on no set schedule, the routine is to purchase a ticket and then wait in line for the next carriage. They stop at the Avenue of Flags where guests may leave the tour to visit Fort Mackinac or the Wings of Mackinac butterfly exhibit (at an additional cost) and then resume their carriage ride on the next available carriage through the area. This is the most convenient way to tour the island. The narrated tour is helpful in understanding the significance of the various island landmarks.

A wheelchair-accessible carriage is available and must be reserved a minimum of one day in advance. Dogs are welcome as long as they do not bark at the horses. Adult fare is $23.50; $9 for children.

Seasons and Events

As many regular visitors will agree, *summer* is the best time to experience the Straits of Mackinac. Most of the businesses and attractions are open during the summer, known blithely by the locals as the "tourist season." Although spring, autumn, and winter each offer some opportunities to get better acquainted with Mackinac, there are many attractions, hotels, and restaurants that close down during the colder months. If you want to experience the best of Mackinac, visit in the summer.

SUMMER

The prime months for visiting are May through August. Temperatures average from a high of 75°F to a low of 47°F. Rainfall is approximately three inches per summer month. Light breezes coming off of the surrounding lakes keep temperatures in this moderate range. Evenings tend to be cool.

MACKINAW MEMORIAL BRIDGE RACE

(Memorial Day ⏁ mackinawcity.com) This is the only competitive race across the Mackinac Bridge. In fact, it is the only time that runners are allowed to run the bridge. Advance registration begins in January.

MEMORIAL DAY PARADE

(Memorial Day ⏁ mackinawmemorialparade.com) This is Michigan's largest Memorial Day parade. It begins at 1:00 p.m. and ends at Colonial Michilimackinac.

COLONIAL MICHILIMACKINAC PAGEANT

(Memorial Day Weekend ⏁ mackinacparks.com) Every year, hundreds of re-enactors bring to life the events of June 2, 1763. On

that day, Native American tribes executed a brilliantly conceived plan to attack the British troops and citizens at the fort. Based on historically accurate accounts, it is the longest running, free Memorial Day pageant in the United States. This is a magnificent production that is truly the highlight of all events for the year. Costuming is historically accurate and collaboration with experts on the time period and nationalities involved brings excellence to the event. Plus, the young men in costume actually play the Native American game of baggataway (an early form of lacrosse). The pageant is performed each afternoon throughout the weekend.

VESPER CRUISE

(*Summer* ↗ *arnoldline.com*) Each Sunday beginning with Father's Day and ending Labor Day weekend, the **Straits Area Resort Ministries** sponsors a 1.5-hour cruise beneath the Mackinac Bridge. Cruises depart from the Arnold Line Ferry docks at 8:00PM. It is a non-denominational event that features gospel music of various types and inspirational talks.

SPRING AND FALL BIKE TOURS

(*June* and *September* ↗ *mackinawchamber.com*) The tours offer various lengths, from 25 miles to 100 miles. They begin at various points along the shore of Lake Michigan and end with a trek across the Mackinac Bridge. This event is repeated in September for a fall color perspective.

Mackinaw City's **Fall Shoreline Scenic Bike Tour** offers a similar experience to the summertime event. Scenic tour routes take riders along the shoreline and through autumn colored woods.

ANTIQUES & CLASSICS ON THE BAY

(*June*) Located on the northern side of the bridge in St. Ignace, this event features restored and original vehicles from 1982 and older. It usually occurs on the third weekend of June.

KITE FESTIVAL

(*June*) The Kite Festival is a fun event for everyone at the Marina Park that takes place during the third week of June. Gorgeous kites of all shapes and sizes fill the skies.

ANNUAL ST. IGNACE CAR SHOW

(*June*) Held the last Saturday of June since 1976, the St. Ignace Car Show is filled with great vehicles, old and new. The event is nationally known and recognized as a quality car event.

MACKINAW CITY FINE ARTS & CRAFTS SHOW

(*June and August*) More than the usual offerings give this show definition. Local licensed trappers display their traditional wares as do woodworkers, basket makers and specialists in Native American handicrafts. The show is held the final weekend in June and in August.

MUSIC IN MACKINAW

(*Summer* ⏱ *mackinachamber.com*) Concerts are offered at 8:00 p.m. every Tuesday and Saturday throughout the summer at Conkling Heritage Park on the waterfront. Bring a chair or blanket to sit on and enjoy the music.

CANADA DAY CELEBRATION

(*July*) July 1st is set aside to celebrate the unique relationship between the United States and Canada. Activities, demonstrations and the like focus particularly on the friendship and shared history of Sault Ste. Marie, Ontario and Mackinaw City.

IRONWORKERS FESTIVAL

(*August*) Friendly competition between ironworkers from both the United States and Canada is the foundation for this weekend event. Competitions include knot tying, rod tying, rivet toss, spud throw and the World Championship Column Climb. The purpose is to honor and recognize those who have spent their lives building nations through their work. Ironwork undergirds skyscrapers and expressways and so much of our lives. These unsung heroes provide structures that we use everyday. The public is invited to join the festival.

CORVETTE CROSSROADS AUTO SHOW

(*August*) The third weekend in August is when hundreds of car enthusiasts come to enjoy this two-day celebration of some of the coolest cars ever built. Events are geared to the celebration of these legendary cars and their devoted fans.

MACKINAC ISLAND LILAC FESTIVAL

(*June* ⌨ *mackinacislandlilacfestival.com*) Ten days of activities feature the island's lush lilacs. Mackinac Island is home to over 100 different varieties as well as some of the oldest lilac bushes in the United States. They bring a profuse glory to the early part of June.

FALL

The fall colors reach their peak about the first week of October. This season is unofficially made up of September, October and November. The weather remains comfortable during September and October with an average daytime temperature of 56°F, falling to an average of 44°F during the night. Precipitation increases to just over 3.5 inches. November weather is unpredictable. Temperatures range from averages of 35°F to 42°F. Temperatures falling into the teens at night are not unheard of. This month tends to be windy and wet. The "wet" may be anything from rain to sleet to snow. For November, be prepared for anything.

FRIDAY NIGHT SOCK HOP

(*Labor Day Weekend*) What better way to start the final weekend of summer than with a good ole' sock hop? The free dance takes place under a big tent at the waterfront park from 7:00 p.m. Until 11:00 p.m. Prizes for the best 1950s costume, a twist contest and other competitions light up the night. A Hot Rod Car Rally brings together the best vehicles of the '50s.

LABOR DAY BRIDGE WALK 🔲

(*Labor Day*) Beginning at 7:00 a.m., the Mackinac Bridge is open to walkers for a traditional walk across the bridge. Ever since the bridge has opened, the walk has commemorated the excitement of bringing the two peninsulas of Michigan together and those who worked so hard to bring it about. The governor often leads off the walk. Buses are available to take transport walkers to St. Ignace to begin their walk. There is a charge for the bus ride, but otherwise this event is free. Safety is a high priority so various rules apply and are regularly reviewed. No bicycles are allowed, and no wagons. Baby strollers and wheelchairs are allowed. This is a huge event and thousands of walkers cross the bridge each year. Wear comfortable shoes, as it is a five-mile trek. The beauty of the straits and the bridge are incredible, especially when viewed from the center of the bridge.

HOPPS OF FUN: A FESTIVAL OF BEER & WINE

(*September*) Brew masters and wine experts gather to educate and inform the thousands of attendees who come to this weekend long event. Over 60 microbrews and 50 Michigan wines are offered for sampling. Live entertainment occurs throughout the festival.

SIDEWALK SALES

(*September*) The second weekend in September has retailers busy marking down their wares for the annual side walk sales. Many stores close for the winter months and this is their final chance to impress shoppers while eliminating inventory. Great deals are in the offering.

RICHARD CRANE MEMORIAL BIG TRUCK PARADE

(September) Semi-trucks come out in force to show off their customized cabs, neon lights and individualized artwork. The "Parade of Lights" takes place at dusk.

FORT FRIGHT

(October ♒ mackinachamber.com) History steps aside for a weekend of mystery as werewolves and other legends roam Colonial Michilimackinac. Have a haunting good time for two nights designed to give "fright" added meaning.

WINTER

The temperatures drop and the snow flies as the winter months of December, January and February unfold. Mackinac Island has an annual snowfall of 112 inches while Mackinaw City has to settle for a more conservative 60-inch covering. Average highs of 26°F and lows of 9°F do not reflect the infamous wind chill factor. This chilly winter accompaniment adds a survivalist feature to the otherwise pristine beauty of the season. Dressing in warm layers is not an option. It is absolutely essential. Careful planning of details for a visit to either Mackinac Island or Mackinaw City is the best protection against dangerous weather. Visitors should plan on using cross-country skis or arranging for taxi service instead of the usual walking tour of the island. It is recommended that a sled be used for transporting luggage and equipment around the snow-covered island.

Mackinac Island is the year-round home to about 500 people. By comparison, Mackinaw City is about triple that amount. Both the island and the Mackinaw City area are laced with trails designated for **cross-country skiing, snowmobiles, sledding** and **snowshoeing**.

Mackinaw City hosts two events during this season: **Winterfest** takes place in mid-January. It is a weekend of fun for the family that includes ice sculpting and other winter activities.

Mackinaw Mush Sled Dog Race is an annual event that happens the first weekend of February. Watch exciting competitions as mushers race for the prize in three-dog, four-dog, six-dog and ten-dog challenges. This is a spectacular weekend involving international racing teams and the opportunity to meet them up close.

THE ICE BRIDGE

Winter at Mackinac Island is exquisite. The straits usually freeze over by February and Lakes Michigan and Huron are covered with ice shortly thereafter. Intrepid islanders use old Christmas trees to line a pathway across the ice to St. Ignace. This ice bridge is used from the time it forms in late January or early February until sometime in March. It brings a welcome relief to the isolation that settles over the island after the holidays.

SPRING

March and April are filled with the fragrance of new life. Wildflowers and other natural flora break through the final remains of winter to begin a new season. The temperatures warm quickly as the anticipation of the full bloom of summer builds.

Businesses are spring-cleaning and putting their final preparations together for their grand openings in May. Guests are welcome after the long winter but few special events are designed for their entertainment. Just being outside in the warmth and color of spring is enough to satisfy anyone. Hiking is the most popular activity during this season of change.

Mackinac Island State Park

About 80 percent of Mackinac Island is designated as the Mackinac Island State Park. Within these approximately 1,800 acres is much of what makes Mackinac Island so special. Forests, trails, unusual geologic formations and some of the most important Mackinac attractions – including **Fort Mackinac** – are located within the park's boundaries.

Established in 1895, the Mackinac Island State Park also has the distinction of being the second area designated as a National Park. (Yellowstone National Park was the first). It was later transferred to the Michigan State Park system. In every direction on Mackinac Island you travel, you either hit the water or hit the Mackinac Island State Park. It is so big, and so important to the region, that visitors almost can't really see Mackinac Island without seeing this park. Though some of the attractions are closed during the off-season, the park itself is open year-round, and offers free admission.

EXPLORING THE PARK

The Mackinac Island State Park offers 70 miles of trails through forest and meadows and along the shoreline. The trails range from novice level on the island circumference to steeper, more challenging paths on the interior. The reward on these trails lies in the uniqueness of the geography and geology that coexist on the island. Trails take hikers, bikers and cross-country skiers past natural monuments like **Arch Rock** and **Sugar Loaf Rock** and through historic battlefields. This is not to minimize the plethora of plant life that fills every inch. Be aware that Mackinac Island hosts one of the largest infestations of poison ivy in Michigan. Keep legs and feet covered while treading these amazing paths.

MACKINAC STATE HISTORIC PARKS

(⌀ mackinacparks.com) In addition to the natural beauty of the Mackinac Island State Park, there are several **Mackinac State Historic Park** sites that form the core of historic attractions on Mackinac Island (and in Mackinaw City). These historic attractions are mostly contained within the park.

Costumed interpreters staff each of the venues. These people are not just decorative fixtures to lend an aura of authenticity – they really enjoy their work and meeting the people that come to visit. Most of these interpreters have studied and love to share their knowledge. Of course, questions are welcomed. Pets on leashes are also welcome. Smoking is allowed only in designated areas of the park with no smoking inside the confines of the various sites.

Admission prices vary according to options selected by the visitor. You can pay a single admission for one site, or buy packages. For those spending some time in Mackinac, the "Triple Choice" ticket is the best. It includes admission to your choice of three **Historic Parks** attractions. The sites are generally open from May through mid-October during the day, with some extended summertime hours.

(For information on the Mackinaw City historic attractions, see the *Historic Mackinaw City* chapter).

FORT MACKINAC **MUST SEE!**

(7127 Huron Rd. ⌀ mackinacparks.com/fort-mackinac/) Fort Mackinac sits on the top of a limestone bluff overlooking Main Street and the straits. The British selected this location because of its superior position of defense. The fort was an active military establishment from 1780 until 1895. The Americans took control of the island and the fort in 1796. Their control was challenged when the British retook the fort in July of 1812 during the first land engagement of the War of 1812. Their intimate knowledge of the island gave the

British advantage over the Americans in this skirmish. Following the resolution of that war, the island was returned to American authority. Re-enactors model life during those final years as an active military installation of the 1880s. Demonstrations primarily focus on military life. They include rifle and cannon demonstrations, military music from the era, parade displays and a court martial. A more recent exhibit explores military medical care and how it changed during the life of the fort.

The site has two entrances. The primary entrance is a long, steep stairway from the street below the fort and up the bluff. There are rest areas along the way. For those with strollers, wheelchairs or who are unenthusiastic about climbing so many stairs, a second entrance is located at the back of the fort via the Avenue of Flags. This entrance is within walking and biking distance along the roadways. It is a pleasant entrance that often is overlooked. Two very different venues offer refreshment inside the fort. The Grand Hotel operates the **Tea Room**, which offers a gourmet lunch selection. The **Food Cart** serves up more traditional picnic foods, snacks and soft drinks.

MCGULPIN HOUSE

(Fort St. and Market St.) The McGulpin House is one of the island's oldest structures, dating from 1780 or earlier. Though not in its original location, this building's primary significance is to showcase a standard home that would have existed during days of fur trading. It is named after William McGulpin, who bought the house in 1819 and lived there with his family. It is an example of early French Canadian architecture. Examples of this architecture style are not often found in such exquisite condition. Visitors will notice various displays that explain the building's structure and overall architectural significance.

BEAUMONT MEMORIAL & AMERICAN FUR COMPANY STORE

(Fort St. and Market St.) This is the original building, restored, of the famous American Fur Company, which was started by John Jacob Astor in 1808. Once again it is stocked as a general store and trading post for the fur industry. Millions of dollars worth of pelts have passed through its door and into the world fur market.

On June 6, 1822 an incident took place here that changed scientific understanding of the human body. French Canadian voyageur Alexis St. Martin was accidentally shot in the stomach at close range. Dr. William Beaumont, the post surgeon at Fort Mackinac, cared for him. St. Martin survived the accident and recovered, but the hole in his stomach never sealed. Through this hole, Dr. Beaumont was able to conduct experiments and discover how the digestive system works in detail previously unknown. He carried his experiments on over a number of years. Incredibly, Alexis St. Martin resumed his life, married and sired multiple children. He lived well into his 80s.

A special room is set aside to detail his story and the impact of Dr. Beaumont's work on medicine and science. This display is constructed with children in mind as well as adults. It is well illustrated and simply told. This presentation style does not embellish or distract from the uniqueness of the story.

THE BIDDLE HOUSE

(End of Market St.) This site was originally the home of Edward Biddle, who arrived at Mackinac in the late 1800s, ready to make his fortune in fur. He married a local Odawa-French Canadian woman named Agatha de la Vigne. In this log cabin, they raised a large family, conducted their business and helped to establish the municipal community on Mackinac Island. Historic interpreters demonstrate life around the hearth as it was in the 1820s.

BENJAMIN BLACKSMITH SHOP

(Next to Biddle House) Mr. Robert Benjamin established the original blacksmith shop in the 1880s. He and his son, Herbert, ran the shop until the 1960s. They fixed the carriage wheels, put shoes on horses and made household goods like hinges for the windows. Later on, they repaired boat engines, lawn mowers and other items while continuing their traditional work. The building was reconstructed in 1970 and houses the original shop contents. Skilled craftsmen offer demonstrations of blacksmithing techniques and products.

STUART HOUSE MUSEUM

(Market St ☎ 906.847.3307) The Stuart House Museum is the original headquarters of John Jacob Astor's American Fur Trading Post. It was built in 1817 and served as the home of the Robert Stuart family and the Ramsey Cooks family. These men served Mr. Astor by running the day-to-day business aspects of the northern outpost. Under their management, the business prospered and over $3 million in furs were shipped from Mackinac in 1822 alone. This was the beginning of the Astor empire, making John Jacob Astor the richest man in the nation and America's first millionaire. The building is owned by the City of Mackinac Island. They are establishing a museum on this site and entrance is by donation. The displays are informative and well done.

AMERICAN FUR COMPANY WAREHOUSE

(Next to Stuart House) An historical marker outside the American Fur Company Warehouse explains the significance of this building; it was here that the actual processing of the pelts happened. Furs from otters, muskrat, mink and beaver were graded as to size, shade of color and fineness of fur before being cleaned, pressed and baled for shipment. Not much remains as evidence of all this industry. Modern use dedicates the first floor as the community

meeting hall. The second floor houses the City of Mackinac Island offices.

MISSION CHURCH

(Main St./Heron St.) Mission Church is the oldest surviving church building in the State of Michigan. Located east of Ste. Anne's on Main Street, it was built in 1829 by Protestant missionary Reverend William Ferry. The Ferrys ministered on the island until the mission became obsolete, due to the demise of the fur industry. Their son later became a United States senator and was responsible for the establishment of Mackinac Island as a National Park. Following their departure, the building was used for various purposes including housing the congregation from Ste. Anne's while they built their church building. Although the use of the structure changed dramatically throughout the years, the structure itself is relatively untouched. It is now owned by the Mackinac Island State Park Commission and has been restored. This is a popular wedding site.

The **Mission House**, located about one block from the Mission Church, is where the work of the Ferrys began. Built in 1825, the Ferrys opened their home as a boarding school to native children. Here, they learned practical skills for surviving in the ever-changing culture around them. These skills included basic academics, farming, tailoring, blacksmithing and homemaking. It currently serves as a staff boarding house for park summer employees. It is not open to the public.

INDIAN DORMITORY

(Main St./Huron St.) In 1836, the Native Americans of the Great Lakes signed the Treaty of Washington and traded their rights to Michigan lands for annual payments. Part of the agreement required that the government build a place where they could stay when they visited the Indian agent to receive their payment. The Indian Dormitory was the fulfillment of that promise. The natives preferred to stay in their own homes on the beach, and thus rarely

actually used the building. It served as a payment distribution center and office for the agent Henry Schoolcraft. From this vantage point, Mr. Schoolcraft studied the natives and compiled information that would lead to a multi-volume work that preserved the ancestry, legends, beliefs and lifestyles of the Great Lakes Native Americans. Published in 1851, his work respectfully treated the native culture. The building is closed to the public, awaiting further renovation.

OTHER HISTORIC SITES

Continuing on Market Street and Main Street, several other outstanding historical sites deserve mention. These are not part of the Fort Mackinac Historic Downtown designations and may have their own entrance fees. Several of these sites still serve as functioning business and municipal offices. Historical markers outside the buildings give insight into the value of the property.

MISSIONARY BARK CHAPEL
(In Marquette Park on Fort St.) The Missionary Bark Chapel is a total recreation based on historical descriptions and drawings. The park is named for the Jesuit priest that established the first European settlement on Mackinac Island. Father Marquette was greatly respected by the Huron people. There is no charge to enter the chapel. It is small and gives a wonderful impression of the closeness of native shelters. A chapel display is located at the front of the building.

TRINITY EPISCOPAL CHURCH
(⌘ trinitymackinac.org) Trinity Episcopal Church is directly opposite of the Bark Chapel. The contrast between the two buildings is astounding. Trinity was built in 1882 to replace the post chapel that

had been converted for military use. It is an active, year-round parish. Entrance is free and respect is appreciated.

STE. ANNE'S CHURCH

(Main St ☎ 906.847.3507 ⌂ steanneschurch.org) Ste. Anne's Church is further east down Main Street. With roots to the original congregation established by Father Marquette, the current building is a replacement of two prior buildings dedicated to Ste. Anne. The first was moved across the ice to a location in downtown Mackinac before being moved one final time to the current site. That structure was replaced in 1874 by the church building now on the location. It was restored to its 1890s appearance in 1996. It is a year-round parish. Entrance is free and respect is appreciated.

MICHIGAN GOVERNORS SUMMER RESIDENCE

(Fort St. Hill & Huron Rd. ☎ 231.436.4100) This 1902 cottage has served Michigan's governors as a summer residence since 1943. Enjoy a tour on Wednesday mornings from June through August.

THE WAR OF 1812 SITES

During the War of 1812, the British captured Fort Mackinac. They did this in a march that began on the far side of the island and cut a path through the middle, straight to the back of the fort. By following Fort Street, off of Main Street, to Huron Road and then a slight turn onto Garrison Road, their path can be retraced. Largely left in its natural state, these sites are recognized with historical markers.

POST CEMETERY

(Near Fort Mackinac) The Post Cemetery features 39 monuments, although about 108 burials took place here. These date from the mid-1820s. The burials included officers, military family members, enlisted men and a few civilians. Most are unknown and a few

graves are unmarked. It was closed to burials with the decommissioning of Fort Mackinac.

FORT HOLMES AND POINT LOOKOUT

(North of the Protestant Cemetery) Established by the British during their invasion, it was originally named Fort George. This is the spot where the British regrouped after their July 16/17 night landing. From here, they had a clear view of the fort and surrounding area. From here, they took the American garrison by surprise and forced their surrender. The view from this point is breathtaking. This spot is 320 feet above lake level and 896 feet above the level of the Atlantic Ocean.

THE BATTLEFIELD

Returning to Garrison Road, continue on to the Four Corners. Here is a crossroad where four roads intersect. Staying on the straight and narrow, Garrison Road becomes British Landing Road at this juncture. To the southwest is the end of the airport runway. In this area is a historical marker marking a battlefield. In this place, the Americans, led by Colonel George Croghan and Major Andrew Holmes, met the British in battle two years after the surrender. They had taken the same path as the British in their maneuver to retake the island. The attempt failed and Major Holmes was among the lives lost that day. Colonel Croghan was forced to retreat. A treaty ended the war in 1815, and the Americans regained Fort Mackinac. Fort George was renamed Fort Holmes in honor of the courage of Major Holmes and the men who were sacrificed in the Battle of Mackinac Island.

BRITISH LANDING

(Along the northwest shore of Mackinac Island) The British Landing site does not look like much but a rocky shore. From this unobtrusive little spot began the first land battle of the War of 1812 and the challenge to the newborn United States of America. Still in recov-

ery mode from the Revolutionary War, America was ill prepared to defend her frontier outposts. This little spot was the beginning of the test of America's resolve to keep what had been gained at so large a price. To ignore this breach onto American territory would have been to invalidate the victories won in the Revolutionary War. The history here is more ideological than practical, but the beauty of the trip to reach this spot is worth the effort.

MACKINAC ROCK FORMATIONS

Having been formed by frozen water and beset on three sides by lakes, the soil of northern Michigan is sandy and rocky. The quantity of sandstone found here attests to the various beaches of the ancient seas. The Mackinaw City area is a flat expanse that edges into the water. Other than the rise of the Headlands, the land is even and lacks the magnificent natural sculptures found on Mackinac Island and the Upper Peninsula. The glacial movement smoothed this land while mounding rocky debris and exposing bedrock in places north and east of "the tip of the mitt."

Limestone, created by the compression and cementing together of the shells of dead sea animals, is the bedrock of Mackinac Island. This white rock, forced up by the turmoil of glacial movement, rises some 300 feet at its highest point above the waters of Lake Huron. The island is three miles long and two miles wide. A circumference of eight miles embraces 2,200 acres. Natural springs are found cascading near the base of the cliffs on the island. Caves and caverns dot the interior. Their hollows are what have remained when the ancient mineral deposits were washed away. They enhance the aura of mystery that legends have garnered for the island.

Formations may be viewed free of charge. No climbing is allowed on any limestone formation. The State Park has forbidden it in an attempt to alleviate man-made destruction of the fragile limestone wonders. Several natural monuments have attracted attention and mesmerized gazers since the island was first visited.

SUGAR LOAF ROCK

(Near Crooked Tree Rd and Sugar Rd junction) Sugar Loaf Rock is a rock "stack" that rises 75 feet from ground level. The name is derived from its shape. The shape of the structure is similar to the birch bark cones that Native Americans used to store maple sugar. Legends claim that it was the wigwam of the Great Gitchi Manitou. Additions to the narrative recall his move from his cherished island to the Northern Lights at the arrival of the Europeans. Another story claims that it is the petrified form of a man who broke a sacred taboo. The man's profile may still be seen. He is a lost soul who can never escape.

ARCH ROCK [MUST SEE]

(Arch Rock Rd near Fort Mackinac) The breccia composition of this arch is rare in the world of natural bridges. Most of these wonders are formed from sturdier materials. Arch Rock on Mackinac Island, 146 feet above water, is made up of limestone cemented together with sandstone. Early geologists predicted its imminent collapse, and they preemptively mourned the loss of it. However, it remains, seemingly uninhibited by the powers of weather on its form.

The desire to preserve this structure played a major part in the decision for Mackinac Island to become a National Park. It gained this status in 1875. It was the second National Park founded. Mackinac Island was transferred to the Michigan State Park system in 1895. Native legend tells us that the sun stood still as it witnessed a beloved Ottawa chief commit a heinous crime. His act brought shame and offense to the Master of Life. He sent powerful wind and turmoil all day. When the sun recovered, it fell from the sky. It blazed through Arch Rock in its astonishment over the sin of the chief. Others claim that Arch Rock is the place where the

Great Gitchi Manitou exited when he removed to the Northern Lights.

The arch stands 146 feet above the eastern shore of the island and is easily reached by taking the shoreline highway. A wooden staircase joins a nature trail to take visitors to the top of the arch.

SKULL CAVE

(1/2 mile north of Fort Mackinac) The renown of this particular feature rests not in the geologic formation but in history. This is the cave where English trader Alexander Henry was secreted by his blood brother following the 1763 massacre at Colonial Michilimackinac. Mr. Henry spent the night on a nest of human bones. This cave and others around the island served as favorite burial spots for the elite in native society. Today, the entrance is roped off out of respect for the generations that received burial there. No bones remain in the cave. It is an interesting site to visit even if one cannot explore the cave's interior.

DEVIL'S KITCHEN

(On M-185, southwest Mackinac Island) This curious name refers to two hollows situated above a larger cavern. Taken together, they appear as a human face with the mouth gaping open. It may be found on M-185 on the island. Native Americans tell us it is the face of bad spirits. Later tales describe them as cannibal spirits. The soot that covers the roofs of these openings is obviously from the fires of these devils. Is that legend or a marketing technique from the late 1800s? No one knows for sure.

Carriage Horses on Mackinac Island *(© Ellen Lively)*

Downtown Mackinac Island *(© Ellen Lively)*

Ferry Ride Across the Straits *(© Ellen Lively)*

Marquette Park *(© Ellen Lively)*

Carriage to the Grand Hotel *(© Ellen Lively)*

Inside the Grand Hotel *(© Ellen Lively)*

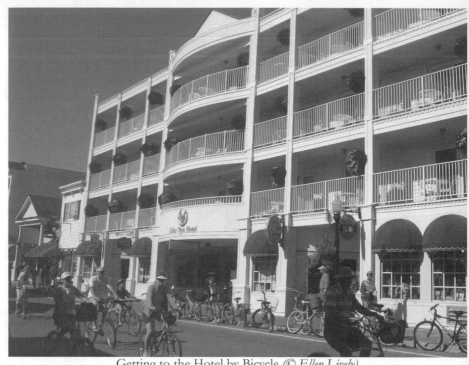

Getting to the Hotel by Bicycle *(© Ellen Lively)*

Fort Mackinac *(© iStockphoto.com/Tom Marvin)*

Old Mackinac Point Lighthouse *(© Ellen Lively)*

Shopping in Mackinaw City *(© Ellen Lively)*

The Docks, Bound for Mackinac Island *(© Ellen Lively)*

Souvenirs *(© Ellen Lively)*

By the Mackinac Bridge *(© Ellen Lively)*

Colonial Michilimackinac *(© Ellen Lively)*

Mackinaw Crossings Shopping Center *(© Ellen Lively)*

Mackinaw City Attractions

Mackinaw City lacks the continuous, far-reaching drama of history that the island boasts. As compensation, they have specialized in making their shore a place where fun memories are made. Not to be outdone, Mackinac Island has invested in its own set of memory-making activities.

Please note that *most* attractions on Mackinac Island and *many* in Mackinaw City are seasonal, so if you're visiting in the winter, call ahead, but be prepared that the attraction is probably closed in winter. The general schedule for seasonal attractions is from May through Labor Day weekend, though some may extend their hours through October.

HISTORIC MACKINAW CITY

Mackinaw City is home to several major historical attractions. The town has also included history markers throughout its districts. The lovely **Walk of History** is found along the waterfront and downtown. Markers along the way inform passersby of people and events that happened on or near that spot. A local artist, Jerry Prior, has carved life-size wooden images of historic personalities. These statues commemorate the contributions that individuals have made. The city has erected them in parks and walkways throughout the area. Plaques detailing the lives of these people are attached.

COLONIAL MICHILIMACKINAC ■MUST SEE■

(102 W. Straits Ave. ⌁ mackinacparks.com/colonial-michilimackinac/)
Colonial Michilimackinac is the nation's longest active archaeological dig, adding new discoveries to the exhibits each season. Reconstructed but authentic buildings showcase period furnishings, interactive displays and exhibits. Re-enactments of colonial life skills

and styles fill the summer months. These include cooking, crafts, a French colonial wedding, voyageur arrivals, games and military demonstrations. The site includes a small Native American encampment and a colonial farm outside of the fort walls. The **Visitors Center Museum Store** offers educational gifts, books and toys next to home décor items.

Colonial Michilimackinac is located on Straits Avenue, west of the Mackinac Bridge. The entrance is through the Visitors Center directly under the bridge.

HISTORIC MILL CREEK DISCOVERY PARK

(9001 U.S. 23 ☞ mackinacparks.com/historic-mill-creek-discovery-park/) An authentic 1790s water-powered sawmill is the anchor of the Mill Creek Discovery Park. It was the ongoing restoration of the mill that provided the lumber for Fort Mackinac on Mackinac Island. In addition to the working sawmill and the accompanying buildings, Mill Creek is a 625-acre nature park with 3.5 miles of trails, most of which are handicap accessible. These trails lead to an active beaver colony and some breathtaking views. A special "Creatures of the Forest" nature program explains the unique habitat that the straits provide for wildlife. New features were added in 2008 that include a 165-foot long Forest Canopy Bridge, a 425-foot Eagle's Flight Zip Line and a Forest Friends Play Area. This is a very family friendly site with something to entertain every age group. Picnicking is encouraged. A refreshment stand on the grounds sells light luncheon fare and treats.

OLD MACKINAC POINT LIGHTHOUSE

(526 North Huron Ave. ☞ mackinacparks.com/old-mackinac-point-lighthouse) Return to the year 1910 with a visit to this museum dedicated to reflect the life of lighthouse keepers on the Great Lakes and especially at the Straits of Mackinac. The maritime exhibits and displays of original artifacts compliment the restored living areas. Interactive displays are easy to use and understand. The original

Fresnel light has been found, and is on exhibit. A trip up the winding stairs allows visitors to experience the daily challenge of a light keeper. From this vantage point, several other lighthouses may be viewed. Many of them are still in operation.

ICEBREAKER MACKINAW MARITIME MUSEUM

(☎ 231.436.9825 ⊕ mackinaw.org) This museum is the home of the recently retired **U.S. Coast Guard Icebreaker Mackinaw**. Located on the railroad dock of South Huron Avenue, the museum details the 62-year history of this vessel as it broke ice on the straits. Tours of the cutter itself offer a glimpse into the world of Great Lakes maritime life and courage. Wear comfortable and secure shoes as the ship has steep ladders, open steel decking and confined spaces. Free hands are a great help in maneuvering around the ship. Daily tours begin in May and last into September. A family pass costs $28, and individually-priced passes are $10 for adults, $6 for youth ages 6 to 17 years. They are closed for Memorial weekend and the first week of June.

MACKINAW CITY WATER FUN

The blue-green waters of the straits constantly lap the shores and beckon guests to join in. In addition to this beguiling invitation to immerse oneself in the waves, there are opportunities to float on, sail over and dive under this wet wonderland. Many **beaches** on both the island and mainland provide access to the sparking water. Swimming shoes are considered necessary protection against the rocky shore and lake bottom. Also, be forewarned that lake swimming is at your own risk. No lifeguards monitor the beaches due to the sheer vastness of the coastline.

THUNDER FALLS FAMILY WATERPARK

(☎ 231.436.6000 ⏱ thunderfallswaterpark.com) As far as waterparks go, Thunder Falls is small. But since it is northern Michigan's only stand-alone outdoor waterpark, there isn't much choice. A dozen water slides, a wave pool, a lazy river, an interactive play area and more make this a great place to spend the day. The attention to safety is impressive. The rock climbing wall, horseshoe pit, volleyball and basketball courts offer a break from the water. Shade and Sun relaxation areas are well planned and comfortable. Thunder Falls is a newer attraction for Mackinaw City and a welcome one. Rates are based on height. Daily and seasonal passes are available. Lockers and towels may be rented daily or seasonally. Food is available at the Thunder Café. Waterpark package may be included with several of the area hotels.

PARASAILING

(☎ 866.436.7144 ⏱ mackinawparasailing.com) If parasailing is your thing, then locations in Mackinaw City, St. Ignace and Mackinac Island give ample opportunity for the experience. Parasailers take off and land from the deck of the boat, so getting wet is at the discretion of the guest. Video and photographic equipment is provided for those who wish to record their escapade. All flights are ten to fifteen minutes long and two heights are offered; 600 ft. and 300 ft. Experienced captains and crews oversee the entire process. Rates are based on single or tandem flying experiences. For the lower altitude, rates for single flyers are $55 and for tandem flyers are $100.

SHEPLER'S LIGHTHOUSE CRUISES

(☎ 231.436.5023 ⏱ sheplersferry.com) Shepler's takes guests onto the waterway for several tour choices that highlight the various lighthouses found on the Straits of Mackinac. Members of the Great Lakes Lighthouse Keepers Association narrate tours. A portion of all proceeds is donated toward preservation and restoration efforts.

Select from a tour to the east of Mackinaw City into Lake Huron with its eight Guardians of the Lakes, and the westward tour into Lake Michigan with its five far-flung sentinels. Other specialty tours may also be available. Base cruise prices are $49.50 per person, children 5-12 years $37.50, children under 5 ride free. Box lunches may be ordered for an additional fee. Pets are not allowed on the cruises. Reservations are recommended.

MACKINAW CITY ATTRACTIONS

Tourists can expect all sorts of attempts to gain their attention and travel dollar. Northern Michigan has had its share of these infamous rip-offs, but few survive today. Some long-standing attractions have more lasting credibility. The smile and chuckle they bring out may end up being the basis of a fond memory in years to come.

CONCERTS ON THE LAWN
(*Summer*) Concerts take place at 8:00 p.m. each Tuesday and Saturday throughout the summer. The Straits Area Concert Band hosts the Tuesday event, while a variety of musical talent fills the Saturday slots. Local donors and sponsors offer these concerts at no charge and the performances are excellent. Concert-goers should bring their own seating for this venue.

JACK PINE LUMBERJACK SHOW
(*U.S. 23, S of Mackinaw City* ☎ *231.436.5225* ⌂ *jackpinelumberjackshows.com*) Jack Pine is a one-of-a-kind opportunity to see real lumberjacks compete in traditional events. The grandstands are covered and shows continue rain or shine from mid-June until Labor Day weekend. Admission is $10 for adults, $8 for seniors and students, $7 for children 14 years and under with toddlers 3 years and

under free. Shows are usually at 7:00 p.m., and 2:00 p.m. shows are sometimes available.

LASER LIGHT SHOW

(Mackinaw Crossings) A laser light show takes place nightly at the Mackinaw Crossings mall. This free event starts at dusk and utilizes state-of-the-art technology to entertain the shoppers.

MACKINAC OLD TIME TROLLEY COMPANY

(☎ 866.651.5474 ⏚ mackinactrolley.com) The Mackinac Old Time Trolley Company offers narrated tours and leaves from many of the hotels in Mackinaw City. The fare of $3 per person takes guests on a historical tour of Mackinaw City. Additional tours include the Mackinaw Pathfinder Tour and the Lake Huron Lighthouses Tour, and are available for groups and individual experiences.

MACKINAW TROLLEY COMPANY TOURS

(☎ 877.858.0357 ⏚ mackinawtrolley.com) Mackinaw Trolley is the original trolley company to operate in Mackinaw City. The experienced guides will lead guests on a Historical tour over the Bridge, St. Ignace, fall color tours, and any number of personalized tours for groups and special occasions. Reservations are recommended. Their tours are handicap accessible.

MAZE OF MIRRORS

(☎ 231.436.7550 ⏚ mirrormazes.com) A life-size maze of glass and mirrors mesmerizes seekers of all ages. The price, however, is steep. The maze takes about 15 minutes to complete at a cost of $10 per adult, less for children. The children especially enjoy this challenge. Coupons are available in the flier stands distributed throughout the area. The Maze of Mirrors is located in the Mackinaw Crossings Mall.

TRAPPERS CREEK ADVENTURE GOLF

(434 Nicolet Ave. ☎ *231.436.5750)* Trappers Creek is an elaborate miniature golf course and amusement center. They take pride in their unique 18-hole course as a well as in their go-kart track and bungee bouncer. Pricing varies according to activity and age. This attraction routinely receives raves from visitors to Mackinaw City.

PARKS NEAR MACKINAW CITY

Bobcats, black bears, coyotes, loons and bald eagles all call the wilderness surrounding Mackinaw City home. For those seeking a more authentic wilderness experience, northern Michigan is comprised of some of the most pristine, untouched wilderness available east of the Mississippi River. Each season offers its own challenges and rewards for those who set out to experience nature at its very best.

Of course, appropriate gear is a survival necessity. Plan on bringing sufficient water, insect repellent and an emergency first aid kit. Clothing should be comfortable and include hardy footwear and a jacket. Being unprepared can turn a wonderful escapade into a nightmare. The key to a successful trip is to plan ahead.

In the wintertime, the Great Outdoors of northern Michigan is a snowmobiler's dream. Ample snow cover allows for maximum time spent on the sleds. Most of the trails that host bikers and hikers during the warm months do double duty as snowmobile trails. Dress in layers for maximum warmth.

THE HEADLANDS

(7725 E Wilderness Park Dr. ☎ *231.436.4051* ᷧ *emmet.mi.us/parkrec)* Approximately two miles west of Mackinac City, on the shores of Lake Michigan, is a region called the Headlands. It is a point of high land jutting out into the water, almost like a mini-peninsula. A nature preserve has been established here that encompasses 550

acres of forest along two miles of shoreline. It is home to a variety of native wildlife and rare, endangered plants. Trails crisscross the Headlands. Hiking, snowshoeing and cross-country skiing are all welcome in the preserve. Nature-lovers from across the globe enjoy encountering the best that nature has to offer here. This is a rugged, beautiful area.

The **McGulpin Lighthouse** has recently been added to the preserve. Built in 1869 and situated on McGulpin Overlook, it predates the lighthouse in Mackinaw City. This piece of land is on record as the first titled property on the straits. The McGulpin family made their living as fishermen for several generations from this spot. They reported weather conditions and ship passages long before the government set up official systems. Even when the lighthouse was decommissioned in 1906, the McGulpins kept up their reporting as a support to the new lighthouse in town. Plans are being made to restore this lovely site and open it to the public.

Marked nature trails and dirt roads crisscross the Headlands. The two miles of shoreline present some glorious views of Lake Michigan. The untouched wilderness boasts rare spring floral and some of the best bird watching in the Midwest.

WILDERNESS STATE PARK
(903 Wilderness Park Drive ☎ 231.436.5381) Thousands of acres await intrepid nature explorers. 250 very rustic camping sites, including some cabins, offer camping in its most natural setting. Beach areas with sand dunes are great swimming spots. A boat ramp provides access to Lake Michigan. Marked trails for hiking, mountain biking and cross-country ski trails lace the park. These trails are generally clearly marked although minimally groomed. Maps to the trail system are available from the park office. There is a vehicle fee required for entrance.

Waugoshaunce Point, at the far western end of Wilderness State Park, is the most remote area of the park. Visitors to this point discover several small islands that are unreachable on foot.

This location is especially entrancing with its wild feel, blue water, glistening sand, and deep forest greens.

FRENCH FARM LAKE

(Emmet County) This undeveloped inland lake sits just two miles southwest of Mackinaw City, and is one of northern Michigan's best-kept secrets. Boats without motors attain superior fishing in the lake. The banning of motor use preserves the clear waters that are home to bass, pike and bluegill. There are few amenities in this 900-acre area. The surrounding trails are a portion of the North Country Hiking Trail that runs from New York to North Dakota. Head south on Wilderness Park Drive, past the Headlands entrance. At road's end, turn left and then an immediate right (before the hill) for the entrance to the park.

MACKINAW CITY RAIL-TRAIL

This rail-trail is the newest addition to the trail system in Michigan. The name is derived from the loose adherence to the railroad system that brought early tourists to Mackinaw City. It covers 62 miles beginning at Gaylord, Michigan and ending in Mackinaw City. It is designed as a multi-use trail with a surface of compressed, crushed limestone that is ten feet wide. It is open for non-motorized use all year. Hikers, bikers and cross-country skiers enjoy this scenic and well-groomed trail. During the winter months, an exception to the non-motorized-vehicle rule is made for snowmobile use from December 1 until March 31. Leaving Mackinaw City, the trail veers east to Cheboygan before turning south towards Mullett Lake. From there it continues south to Burt Lake in Indian River. The trail then continues on to Gaylord.

CANOEING, KAYAKING, FISHING AND BOATING

All sorts of inlets, streams and small lakes are located in northern Michigan. For those visiting the Straits of Mackinac area, **Cecil Bay**, west of Mackinaw City, is an inviting waterfront. Small islands dot the bay. These are best visited with a canoe or kayak. Three smaller bays are located within the main bay. **Big Stone Bay** is noted for fishing, and **Trails End Bay** is a great spot to explore. Cecil Bay does have a boat launch located within Wilderness State Park. The United States Coast Guard is very active in this area. All safety measures should be strictly adhered to for the sake of all on the waterways.

Carp/Paradise Lake is one lake with two names. Originally known as Carp Lake, it home to excellent fishing. As time passed, residents sought to appeal to the tourists that passed through. They petitioned and changed the name to the more aesthetic "Paradise Lake." Either way, the lake is good for fishing and boating. Launch ramps are located on U.S. 31. A small town has grown up on the edge of the lake. The town provides the necessary amenities for a successful day on the water.

Did you know... ?

*The **Mackinac Island State Park** encompasses about 80% of Mackinac Island.*

Other Attractions

Tours, museums, an insect museum and a butterfly conservatory all have their places on Mackinac Island. Visiting the town on Mackinac Island – not just the State Park – add to the area's historical and natural beauty, and can be a lot of fun. The region has several golf courses as well.

MACKINAC ISLAND

Though Mackinaw City is the place to be for goofy tourist fare, Mackinac Island has a few offbeat oddities vying for your tourist dollar. The Mackinac Island State Park is by far the most popular attraction in Mackinac.

MACKINAW BREEZE CATAMARAN SAILING
(☎ 906.847.8669 ᵀ *mackinacbreeze.com*) Sailing brings the experience of sailing the freshwater seas in the Mackinac Island vicinity to guests on a daily basis. The boats are docked near the Mackinac Marina. Weather permitting, they venture onto the waters that many professional sailors feel rival the oceans in their beauty and complexity. Guests are welcome to assist the captain and crew trim the sails or to sit back and relax. Sailing times are usually planned for the afternoon.

A typical tour requires one and a half hours to circumnavigate the island. Private charters, including the popular Harbor History Tours, are available for private or group events. Reservations are recommended but not required. The vessel is Coast Guard certified. Rates for adults are $30; children under 13 years are $15 except for evening cruises when their rate is equal to the adult charge. Please wear soft-soled shoes.

MACKINAC ISLAND BUTTERFLY HOUSE & INSECT MUSEUM

(☎ 906.847.3972 ⊕ originalbutterflyhouse.com) This museum is the first of its kind in Michigan, and the third oldest in the nation. Their tropical gardens include ponds and waterfalls that are home to toads, turtles and fish. Interactive displays educate and entertain at the same time. The Insect Museum is home to the current record holder for the "world's heaviest bug." At any given time, 800 individual butterflies reside at the house with a variety range of 50-100 different species. This is the original complex and they are proud of their heritage on Mackinac Island.

Adult fees are $7.50; children ages 4-11 years are $4; toddlers 3 years and under are admitted at no charge. The facility is wheelchair and stroller friendly but no animals are allowed.

WINGS OF MACKINAC BUTTERFLY CONSERVATORY

(☎ 906.847.WING ⊕ wingsofmackinac.com) This lovely glass conservatory is home to an average of 80 different varieties of butterflies on any given day. They are housed in an exquisite garden setting. Four hundred butterflies a week live out their life spans in this protected setting. Curators are on hand to monitor their care and answer any questions that guests may have. Beautiful, educational and fun, this is like an oasis. Cost is $6 per adult and $3 for children.

PROFESSOR HARRY'S OLD TIME PHOTOS

(Star Line Boat Dock in the Orphan Corner Mall ☎ 906.847.6000) Professor Harry's puts visitors into the historic picture, literally. They have meticulously studied antique photography and era costuming in order to produce historically accurate images. The owners construct many of the costumes themselves. Costumes slip over street clothes and they promise to fit anyone that desires a photo setting. The photographs are delivered in about ten minutes. Reprints are available by mail. They do an expert job. No appointment is necessary.

THE HAUNTED THEATRE

(Near Shepler's ☎ *231.818.0527* ⌁ *mackinacislandhauntedtheatre.com)* The Haunted Theatre is both a haunted house and a wax monster museum. They claim authentic hauntings because the attraction is built on a former Native American ancestral burial ground. Artists and engineers created the wax monsters, with life-like movement and visage. Based upon the native legends, Mackinac Island monsters join some more worldly counterparts such as the Phantom of the Opera. Visitors usually leave at a quick pace with nervous laughter. The same $6 price applies to every guest.

GOLF

Golfing, of course, is the grand exception to Mackinac's emphasis on nature. Instead of leaving nature alone, area golf courses set themselves apart like emerald jewels. They have been designed by professionals in the field and rank among some of the best in the world.

MACKINAW CLUB

(☎ *231.537.4955* ⌁ *mackinawclub.com)* The Mackinaw Club is located four miles south of Mackinaw City. This 18-hole, par 72 course was designed by golf designer Jerry Matthews on 310 acres. They are open May through October. Rates are in the $25 - $40 range for 18 holes with a cart. They are subject to change due to time of season with August rates being the highest. It is open to the public.

THE JEWEL

(Grand Hotel, Mackinac Island ☎ *800.334.7263* ⌁ *grandhotel.com)* The Jewel is on the interior of Mackinac Island, at the Grand Hotel. Opened in 1901, the original 9-hole course, named the Grand, was

redesigned in 1984. Golf course architect Jerry Matthews designed a nine-hole addition titled "The Woods" in 1994. Hotel guests can play 18 holes of exceptional golf, with a cart, for $90 (or $120 for non-hotel guests).

WAWASHKAMO GOLF CLUB

(☎ 906.847.3871 *⌘ wawashkamo.com*) The Wawashkamo Golf Club is Michigan's longest, continually operated, unchanged golf course. Scottish golf pro Alex Smith designed the course in 1898 using natural hazards. They also offer a comprehensive "Junior Program" and lessons. The public is welcome to enjoy this facility. A game with 18 holes and a cart is $65; a nine-hole game is available (with cart) for $45. Reservations are encouraged.

Did you know… ?

*During the winter an **ice bridge** sometimes forms, allowing people to walk to Mackinac Island.*

Shopping

In Mackinac, no huge covered malls with their acres of parking lots blemish the landscape. Chain department stores have yet to discover the retail market on the Straits of Mackinac. This is just fine with area shop owners. Local residents take pride in their individualized offerings to shoppers. Mackinaw City favors stores that specialize in meeting the interests of particular groups of shoppers. They also feature the trademark tourist shops filled with tee shirts and plastic souvenirs. Mackinac Island focuses on the more upscale needs of purchasers with its specialty boutiques. A few tourist shops are sprinkled across the Mackinac Island downtown in recognition of the variety of clientele that visit. It all adds up to a good time with a lot of choices. Those shops included in this section are a sampling of retail venues available.

FUDGE

During the mid-1800s, Mackinac Island received an influx of visitors as people immigrated towards the north and west. The wealthy came as vacationers who were beginning to appreciate the island for its beauty and healthful atmosphere. The island responded by building tourist facilities as quickly as possible.

Armed with an English fudge recipe dating from the 1830s, Henry F. Murdick and his son, Newton Jerome, left their original trade behind in the Port Huron, Michigan area. They risked everything to be the first confectionery shop on Mackinac Island. They opened for business in 1887, the same year that the Grand Hotel began welcoming guests. Their gamble paid off as they provided treats to sailors and passengers.

Detroit caramel-corn makers Harry and Ethel Ryba opened their first Mackinac Island fudge shop with fresh enthusiasm in 1960. Harry had a reputation of aggressive salesmanship and this skill became the turning point that saved the tradition of Mackinac

Island fudge. One of his first moves was to install a ventilation system that effused the delightful aroma out into the streets. He also moved the fudge-making tables into the front windows where customers could watch the hot fudge being paddled before it was shaped into loaves. Customers responded well to these invitations. They were also the first to offer their product in a variety of specialty flavors.

Today, fudge shops in Mackinaw City and Mackinac Island beckon travelers. It is part of the tradition and modern lore of the straits. It is a piece of fun that has grown up with tourism at Mackinac Island and the straits. Taste test at every shop, pick a favorite and splurge on a pound of decadence to take home.

MACKINAW CITY

Shopping in Mackinaw City is almost strictly of the souvenir fare. Though there are the occasional diamonds in the rough, expect to see a wide array of t-shirts, coffee mugs, collectibles, and other non-necessities that in some way say "I've been to Mackinaw."

THE MACKINAW CROSSINGS MALL
(248 South Huron Ave ☎ *231.436.5030 ⌀ mackinawcrossings.com)* The Mackinaw Crossings is an outdoor mall that takes storybook Main Street as its theme. Storefronts have a themed, tourist-centric quality to them. Inside, the boutiques and shops specialize in out-of-the-ordinary wares. More than 50 stores fill the mall.

Central Avenue is the main street of Mackinaw City. Most of the shopping opportunities line its red brick sidewalks. The selections given here are a sampling of the variety.

THE BEAR COMPANY OF MACKINAW CITY
(200 S. Nicolet Ave. ☎ *231.436.9944)* The Bear Company offers 5,000 square feet of souvenirs and a wide range of random items

for sale. Next to the obligatory tourist souvenirs are selections that include apparel, swim wear and accessories.

CANDY CORNER & WINDJAMMER GIFTS

(331 E. Central Ave. ☎ *231.436.5591)* Candy Corner is a two-story shop that is open all year. They offer confections that include fudge, caramel corn and ice cream. Sugar free items are also available. Souvenirs of all sorts and pricing have found their way to this shop.

COFFMAN HARDWARE & CAMP STORE

(227 E Central Ave. ☎ *231.436.5650* ⌂ *coffmancaseknives.com)* A very practical store for the outdoorsman, this is the place to obtain Michigan fishing and hunting license, bait, and all of those related items. Bike repair is offered as well. Open 7 days all year.

ENCHANTED KNIGHTS

(230 E. Central Ave. ☎ *231.436.4059* ⌂ *enchantedknights.com)* Located in the Mackinaw Crossing Mall, they specialize in all things medieval, mythological and legendary.

HUSH PUPPIES & FAMILY

(402 S Huron St. ☎ *231.436.5321)* They offer quality footwear all year long with a good selection of sizes and styles.

ISLAND BOOKSTORE - COFFEE SHOP

(215 E. Central Ave. ☎ *231.436.2665* ⌂ *islandbookstore.com)* This full service bookstore celebrates its status as Mackinaw City's premier bookstore with excellent service and quality selections that include magazines, newspaper, toys, and gifts alongside of their books.

MACKINAC BAY TRADING COMPANY

(☎ *231.436.5005)* This is the closest thing to an indoor mall in the region. They fill 24,000 square feet with a fudge shop, wine tasting

room, Nonna Lisa's Ristorante, lodge style furniture and the **Mackinac Bay Build Your Bear Workshop** for toy-lovers.

MACKINAW CLOTHING COMPANY

(319 E. Central Ave. ☎ *231.436.5093)* This is a wonderful shop. They cater to the need for real, quality clothing for the entire family and not tourist fare. Open all year, they feature selections from national brands. Their prices are reasonable. Helpful salespeople enjoy giving good service to shoppers.

MACKINAW KITE COMPANY

(☎ *231.436.8051* *mackinawkiteco.com)* Every kind of kite imaginable may be found here. This is an amazing store. They offer kite demonstrations throughout the summer at the waterfront. It is hard to resist making a purchase here.

PAWS FUR FUN

(182 South Huron Ave. ☎ *231.436.5700)* Located in Mackinaw Crossings, this store has gifts and treats for dogs, cats, horses and people. The imagination behind some of these gifts is worth taking the time to visit this cute shop.

RAINBOW SPORTSWEAR

(317 E. Central Ave. ☎ *231.436.5631)* They refer to themselves as the tee shirt hub of Mackinaw and offer personalizing while you wait. In addition to the shirts, it the largest selection of belt buckles in the country. Genuine leather belts may be custom fitted. Additional leather goods, knives and gift items are available.

SOUVENIRS MARUGO

(226 E. Central Ave. ☎ *231.436.6278)* This tourist souvenir store truly stands out from the rest. Knives, swords, daggers, throwing stars and gun replicas adorn their walls. Other unique items make

this a fun place to spend time. They advertise the best prices in town and they fulfill that promise on most items.

TEYSEN'S GALLERY & HOME ACCENTS

(300 E. Central Ave. ☎ *231.436.7519* ✆ *teysens.com)* Teysen's is a family-owned operation that has set the standard for a quality shopping experience in Mackinaw City. They specialize in local, artistic crafts, which gives them a unique array of items. Prices are reasonable, especially considering the quality and service that accompany each purchase.

TEYSEN'S GIFT SHOP & TEYSEN'S MOCCASIN SHOP

(☎ *231.436.7011* ✆ *teysens.com)* Grab a pen and some paper – this is a great place to make a wish list. There are so many interesting things in these two stores. The gift shop sells beautiful jewelry, specialty candles and the like. They are one of the largest Minnetonka dealers in the state. But the leather merchandise goes far beyond moccasins. Exquisite purses, boot and foot wear rival the offerings in Texas.

TOP HATS OF MACKINAW

(224 S. Huron St. ☎ *231.436.4000)* Kids cannot resist this shop. From the classic to the quirky, hats of every kind fill the shelves. They specialize in quality, name brand head gear with a smattering of fun for good measure.

TWISTED CRYSTAL

(301 E. Central Ave. ☎ *231.436.7020* ✆ *twistedcrystal.com)* Gorgeous, handcrafted jewelry in a boutique setting, this store also features original wire sculpted designs. Natural and local stones are used including the Petoskey Stone and Lake Superior Agates. A must see!

NASCAR / SPEEDWAY STORE
All things related to the famous racing sport are available here. Located in the Mackinaw Crossings Mall.

MACKINAC ISLAND

Boutiques, art galleries and shops fill every nook and cranny of the downtown area. Side streets bustle with their share of storefronts as well. The variety is extraordinary with an emphasis on the artistic, the historical and all of the finer things in life.

The two resort properties, Grand Hotel and Mission Point Resort, house their own shopping opportunities. From simple shops like newsstands to upscale, full service clothiers, they are prepared to meet the need and whimsy of guests. The public is welcome to visit their shops although a fee may be charged to gain entrance to the resort.

A few shops offer the standard tourist souvenir selections. As with everything on the island, shops display with flair and style. Clothing stores, antiques shops, art galleries, and more crowd the streets. An entire day could be spent simply browsing and discovering all of the shops on Mackinac Island. There are far too many stores to detail here. The selection given is a taste test of sorts to pique the interest of those headed for a shopping excursion on the island.

BALSAM SHOP
(On Main St. ☎ *906.847.3591* ✆ *balsamshop.com)* The Balsam Shop has established itself as a connoisseur of American made gifts. A smattering of tourist tee shirts and sweatshirts join the maple syrup treats, silver and copper jewelry and other unique gifts. They have two different locations.

MACKINAC LAPIDARY

(On Market St. ☎ 906.847.1040 ⏏ mackinaclapidary.com) Like a second home for the owner/creator of the fine jewelry found here, he creates custom jewelry as guests to his store look on. This is a fascinating place to stop. Adjoining the lapidary is a bead shop where guests may design their own creations. A very well-organized working area is surrounded by beads from all over the world.

GREAT TURTLE TOYS

(1460 Main St. ☎ 906.847.6118 ⏏ greatturtletoys.com) This company employs three locations to display their wares. Kids of all ages enjoy stopping in for a demonstration and to play with the products. This interaction with the toys before purchase is encouraged. The toy selection is high quality with an emphasis on education made fun. Sales representatives are skilled in product knowledge and demonstration.

ISLAND BOOKSTORE

(On Main St. ☎ 888.421.READ ⏏ islandbookstore.com) The Island Bookstore is a full-service bookstore that goes above and beyond the ordinary in their service and selections. They specialize in books about the Mackinac area and their website gives an excellent overview of their stock.

LILAC AND LACE

(On Market St. ☎ 906.874.0100 ⏏ lilacsandlace.com) Lilac and Lace offers several locations on the island. Market Street hosts their downtown store. They consider themselves the first art gallery on the island. In this tradition, they present original works in a variety of art mediums. Oil, watercolors and acrylic paintings adorn the walls. Hand blown glass sits amid custom jewelry and fine china tea sets. It is a lovely store to visit.

Dining

Many local menus feature the perennial favorite of the Great Lakes, the whitefish. The earliest records describe this tasty fish and the methods used to prepare it. It was a staple of the native diet. It was prized not only for its easy attainment but because it really is delicious. Planked whitefish is the most historic method of preparation followed by smoking. While natives with fishing nets and canoes are no longer the backbone of the fishing industry, the laws and oversight have protected the fish in these waters from extinction. Generations to come will share in this age-old delicacy.

Dining in the Mackinac Area is as much about making each guest feel welcome and valued as it is about filling that gnawing hunger. Service is regarded as an art and an intricate component of the dining experience. While perfection may not be achieved every time, it is the heartbeat of Mackinac area restaurateurs.

THE PASTIE

The northern Michigan pastie (pronounced with the short "a" sound) is the stuff legends are made of. The name comes from a colloquialism of the word "pastry." Several ethnic groups claim the pastie as their unique contribution. After sifting through the myriad tales and records, one claim stands out.

Pasties came to the area with the Cornish miners who were headed for the copper and iron mines of the Upper Peninsula. Housewives made a crust and filled it as they would fill a turnover pie. Instead of a sweet filling, they used leftovers from the evening meal. This usually was a combination of meat, potatoes, carrots, rutabaga and/or turnips. After seasoning, the dough was folded over and sealed. Leftover pastry was formed into initials that designated the pastie's intended recipient. Finally, it was popped into the oven to bake. By the time it was finished, those leaving for work were ready to go. The hot pastie was carefully wrapped to help retain the heat. Miners would leave their wrapped, hot lunches at the mine entrance. This helped ensure that workers were accounted for and that everyone ate his own homemade feast.

Today, pasties are served with various meat choices, topped with gravy and sour cream. No, it is not a dieter's dream food but it is wonderfully good. Some chefs have experimented with vegetarian versions that rival the meaty versions in taste. The locals consider this as part of the "up north experience" and all visitors are encouraged to give this original a try.

MACKINAW CITY

Mackinaw City is not the place to rely on the tried and true fast food favorites. The "Golden Arches" have not found their way to the tip of Michigan's Lower Peninsula. Dairy Queen, Burger King, Subway and Kentucky Fried Chicken are the only national fast food chains that have made the trek to the area. Instead, the good people of Mackinaw City have created some fine alternatives of their own to satisfy the hungry folks that visit their town. Eateries here are less concerned with an haute couture dining experience than in offering travelers a solid, comforting meal at a reasonable cost. Following a busy day of romping in the water or collecting memories at the local attractions, a hardy meal of favorites is often the "piece de resistance" to end the day right.

Restaurants are open from May through October unless noted otherwise with **AY** (all year). Michigan law requires non-smoking sections. **NS** designates an entirely smoke-free establishment, **AB** for alcoholic beverages available, **CM** for special children's menu offered. For specific *pricing information*, please contact the establishment directly.

ADMIRAL'S TABLE

(502 S Huron St. ☎ *231.436.5687)* A hearty breakfast menu at Admiral's Table features a breakfast buffet. A nice selection of salads and sandwiches are available for lunch. Dinner features include steaks, chicken fish and daily specials.

ANNA'S BUFFET

(416 S Huron St. ☎ *231.436.5195* ✆ *mackinawdining.com)* Anna's claims the largest buffet in the city, which is open for all meals. A substantial menu backs up the buffet. Good for quick feeding of really large groups (such as bus tours).

AUDIE'S CHIPPEWA ROOM

(314 N Nicolet St. ☎ *231.436.5744* ✆ *audies.com)* Audie's **Chippewa Room** is a great place to eat. The food is excellent and the atmosphere distinctive. Native American décor mixed with local artifacts add to the ambiance. The chef is a graduate of the Culinary Institute of America and the owners give his creativity free reign. This is one of the nicer places in town and well worth the visit. They have the largest wine list in the city. The restaurant is located at the base of the Mackinac Bridge. Featured entrees include vegetarian, seafood, rack of lamb, steaks and whitefish. AB, CM

Audie's Family Restaurant is open year round for all meals. Another great choice, this is the more family-friendly version of the Chippewa Room. Burgers, steaks, fish and BBQ ribs lead this menu. They offer a senior discount. AB, CM, AY

B.C. PIZZA

(209 E Central Ave. ☎ *231.436.5500)* "B.C." stands for "Best Choice." They are not shy about how much they believe in their product or how much they aim to please their customers. A pizza and salad bar offer is available for customers choosing to dine in. Children six years old and under eat free with a paying adult. Salads, subs and wraps are all on the menu next to the Select, Specialty

and Deluxe pizzas. Daily specials are available for both dine in and carry out customers. B.C. delivers to a limited area with a minimum order requirement. AY (but weekend-only in the winter)

BIG BOY RESTAURANT

(404 Nicolet St. ☎ 231.436.5021) Located on the south side of town, Big Boy is easily accessed from the main route into the city. They offer the signature Big Boy menu of sandwiches, desserts and dinner choices. Their malts and shakes are some of the best in town. CM, AY

BLUE WATER GRILL & BAR

(918 S Huron St. ☎ 231.436.7818) It has been said that bars serve the best burgers. Blue Water Grill & Bar features steaks, pasta and seafood along with their burgers. AB

CUNNINGHAM'S FAMILY RESTAURANT

(312 E Central Ave. ☎ 231.436.8821) Cunningham's features a huge menu, and specialize in pasties. Regular vacationers to Mackinaw City often include family traditions that include at least one meal here. Consistent quality and service creates this kind of following. Their chicken pasties in particular draw rave reviews. CM, NS

DARROW'S FAMILY RESTAURANT **MUST SEE**

(301 Louvigny St. ☎ 231.436.5514) Darrow's takes a little determination to find. The restaurant is located west of the I-75 overpass and is well worth the effort as it is hands-down the best meal in town. Everything is made from scratch. Gorgeous homemade pies that taste even better than they look are created daily. The owners are highly involved as is the entire family. CM, NS, AY

DIXIE SALOON FOOD & SPIRITS

(Corner of Huron & Central ☎ *231.436.5005)* Dixie Saloon does things in a big way. Large portions of steaks, ribs and burgers are served in the grand, two-story log building. Live music and dancing earn them the reputation of being "Mackinaw City's Hot Spot." AB, AY

EMBERS RESTAURANT

(810 S. Huron St. ☎ *231.436.5773)* 35 years of experience entitles Embers to claim the best buffet in Mackinaw City. A full menu of entrees fills out their offerings. They have developed both the buffet and menu from all of their experience. AB

THE HISTORIC DEPOT

(Mackinaw Crossings ☎ *231.436.7060)* At The Historic Depot, you can choose to dine in the casual dining room or in the open-air café. Sandwiches, seafood, steaks and BBQ ribs head their menu. It is a nice place to relax in the middle of shopping at Mackinaw Crossings. CM, AB

JR.'S TAILGATE PUB & TWO AMIGOS'S MEXICAN KITCHEN

(101 E Central Ave. ☎ *231.436.8540)* Two Amigos is the only place in town for good Mexican food. They offer dinner from 4 p.m. until midnight. Karaoke, live entertainment, pool and darts make this an all-evening place. AB

LIGHTHOUSE RESTAURANT

(618 S Huron St. ☎ *231.436.5191* ⌨ *mackinawdining.com)* Fish, steaks, chicken, pasta; they do it all nicely at Lighthouse Restaurant. Fine dining presented in a casual atmosphere. They also offer a full service lounge. CM, AB

MACKINAW PASTIE & COOKIE CO.

(514 S Huron St./117 W Jamet ☎ *231.436.5113/231.436.8202)* Two locations bring forty-three years of making the best pasties and cookies in the city. Mackinaw Pastie has been featured on the *Detroit News* "Michigan's Best" list for five years running. Their menu is specialized; they know what they do best and they do it consistently. Stock up on the cookies, they make wonderful snacking anywhere, anytime.

MAMA MIA'S PIZZERIA & RESTAURANT

(231 Central Ave. ☎ *231.436.5534)* Build your own favorite pizza or order from the menu. The menu features Mexican selections next to pizzeria subs and sandwiches. Specialty pizzas include taco, fajita and Hawaiian choices. Mama Mia's is a busy, determined place. They were devastated by fire a few years back and came out of it bigger and better than before. AB

MANCINO'S OF MACKINAW CITY

(717 Nicolet St. ☎ *231.436.7474)* Located just south of town, Mancino's draws local customers year round with their selection of 22 sandwiches and pizza. Their grinders are definitely worth the drive. They also offer soft serve ice cream, sundaes and shakes. There is limited dining space, but excellent for carryout. AY

'NEATH THE BIRCHES

(14277 Mackinaw Hwy U.S. 31 ☎ *231.436.5401* ⌨ *mackinawdining.com)* There are several interesting things about this restaurant. First of all, the same cook, Marvel Jones, has been in the kitchen turning out perfect steaks, chops and fish for over 39 years, and she has no intention of retiring and leaving the cooking to less experienced hands. Secondly, the location is (as the name describes) beneath some beautiful birch trees on the outskirts of town. The windows overlook a lovely area that is favored by wild turkeys, birds, raccoons and other wildlife. Finally, of course, is the food.

The homemade pies and Mrs. Jones' attention to detail in her work make this a favorite of area residents. AB, AY

NONNA LISA'S

(312 S Huron St. ☎ *231.436.5005)* Authentic Italian food can be found in this eatery located in back of the Mackinac Bay Trading Company. 12-inch wood-fired personal pizzas dominate this fine dining establishment. Paninis, strombolis, homemade authentic desserts, and other Italian choices are available. Low-carb options are offered for those who desire the best taste without sacrificing diet requirements. CM, AB

O'REILLYS IRISH PUB & RESTAURANT

(401 E Central Ave. ☎ *231.420.7144)* The only Irish pub in the area has all the excitement that is expected. Nightly entertainment includes karaoke, bands, and comedians. Rotisserie chicken, burgers and fish are offered on the menu. They rival Dixie's Saloon for the title of "Hot Spot." AB, AY

PANCAKE CHEF

(327 E Central Ave. ☎ *231.436.5578)* At Pancake Chef, family dining is offered year round at a reasonable price, with great service. Breakfast is served all day. Lunch and dinner menus suggest traditional American fare with a few tasty surprises thrown in for good measure. Salad bar, breakfast and dinner buffet are the most attractive options. CM, AY

PALACE RESTAURANT & PIZZA

(316 E Central Ave. ☎ *231.436.5788/231.436.5462)* A full menu with daily specials compliments the specialties of pizza and pasties. Palace Restaurant has been twice voted "best in northern Michigan" for these food items in particular. They deliver good food and good service; delivery is also available. CM, AB

SCALAWAGS WHITEFISH & CHIPS

(226 E Central Ave. ☎ *231.436.7777* ✆ *scalawagswhitefish.com)* Pass the malt vinegar! Tasty traditional fish and chips baskets take on new definition when prepared at Scalawags. Whitefish is the featured fish but customers make their selection from a variety of fresh Great Lakes fish including perch and walleye. Even better news is the fact that they use no trans fat oils in the interest of better health for their clientele. They also offer outdoor seating. CM

MACKINAC ISLAND

Dining on Mackinac Island is different than dining on the mainland. Restaurants here seek to please the most discerning palette and satisfy the slightest taste whim of every guest to the island. Common meals such as pizza or hamburgers are not just good on Mackinac Island; they are excellent. The island does not look to prepackaged food items to assist them in their hospitality. They seek out the finest ingredients and create their own offerings. Other than Starbucks, there are no national food chain restaurants. Islanders prefer to create meals and treats that help make a visit to their island a satisfying and memorable experience.

Restaurants are open from May through October unless noted otherwise with **AY** (all year). The main body of eateries is located in the downtown area on Main Street. Specific notations concerning location are given when necessary. Michigan law requires non-smoking sections. **NS** designates an entirely smoke-free establishment, **AB** for alcoholic beverages available, **V** for vegetarian entrees available, **CM** for special children's menu offered.

Price range is indicated as follows: *$ = inexpensive, $10 or less, $$ = moderate, $10 - $20, $$$ = expensive, $20 - $40 or more.*

1852 GRILL ROOM

(Island House Hotel ☎ *906.847.3347)* The 1852 Grill Room is a wonderful steak house that offers pasta and fine vegetarian entrees as well. Outdoor seating and entertainment are offered. AB, CM, V ($$$)

ASTOR STREET CAFE

(On Astor St. ☎ *906.847.6031)* Astor Street Café offers home cooking at its best with soups, salads, gourmet sandwiches and pasties offered, along with American traditions of roast beef or turkey dinners, meatloaf and fresh fish. CM ($)

BISTRO ON THE GREENS

(Mission Point Resort ☎   *906.847.3312)* This Bistro serves breakfast, lunch and dinner overlooking the putting greens at the Mission Point Resort. The outdoor seating area is pet friendly. AB, CM, V ($$$)

CANNONBALL DRIVE-IN

(Shoreline Rd. ☎ *906.847.0932* ⏚ *cannonballmackinacisland.com)* Located on Shoreline Road, half way around the island at British Landing, Cannonball is a great place to stop while biking around the Island. Try their famous fried pickles or select from their menu of burgers, hot dogs, ice cream and snacks. They sell cold bottled water to replenish thirsty bikers. CM, V ($)

CARLETON'S TEA SHOP

(Grand Hotel ☎ *906.847.3331)* Located within the Grand Hotel, Carleton's serves lunch, afternoon tea along with coffee and gorgeous desserts. NS ($$)

CARRIAGE HOUSE

(Hotel Iroquois ☎ *906.847.3321)* Gourmet breakfast, lunch and dinner of inspired American cuisine are offered at the Carriage House,

at the Hotel Iroquois, with indoor and outdoor seating available. Reservations are suggested. V, AB, CM, NS ($$$)

CHILLIN' AND GRILLIN' WATERFRONT CAFE

(On Arnold Dock ☎ *906.847.6177)* Located on the dock of the Arnold Ferry, Chilli' and Grillin' serves fresh fish baskets as well as traditional grill favorites. V, CM ($)

CUDAHY ROOM INN AT STONECLIFFE

(☎ *906.847.3355)* The Cudahy Room at Stonecliffe is the only restaurant located on this side of the island. Reservations are strongly suggested as they have limited seating and high demand for their excellent menu. V, AB, CM ($$)

DOG HOUSE

(At Windermere Pt ☎ *906.847.6586)* This outdoor gazebo serves up hot dogs and brats topped with chili, kraut and a myriad of other choices. Ice cream cools it all down. ($)

DOUD'S MARKET

(7260 Main St. ☎ *906.847.3444* ✆ *doudsmarket.com)* Michigan's oldest family-owned grocery store makes some of the best pizza on the island. Additional menu items are gourmet sandwiches from their suggested menu, or you can build your own meal. AY ($)

EPICUREAN

(At Mission Point ☎ *906.847.3312)* Epicurean is the signature restaurant for Mission Point Resort. Gourmet fare is offered from a range of international cuisines. Live piano music nightly completes the experience. AB, V, CM ($$$)

ESPRESSO CAFE

(At the Inn on Mackinac ☎ *906.847.6348)* The Espresso Café is a coffee house that puts national chains to the test. The establish-

ment provides a variety of coffee beverages and light luncheon offerings. V ($)

FORT MACKINAC TEA ROOM

(At Fort Mackinac ☎ *906.847.3328)* This is a Grand Hotel Restaurant located within Fort Mackinac. Meals are served on an outdoor patio the bluff overlooking the fort's gardens and island waterfront. The Tea Room serves full lunch and dinner entrees. V, CM, AB ($)

FRED'S DELI

(Shepler's Ferry Docks ☎ *906.847.3240)* Fred's Deli takes no shortcuts in their food preparation. They offer hand cut French fries, fresh squeezed lemonade, burgers, shakes and ice cream. V, CM ($)

GATE HOUSE

(Across from Little Stone Church ☎ *906.847.3331)* The Gate House the newest Grand Hotel Restaurant. Watch sports on the large screen televisions or enjoy the outdoor seating. A casual grill menu with regional specialties is served. AB, CM, V ($$/$$$)

GOODFELLOWS GRILL

(Lake View Hotel ☎ *906.847.0270)* American and Italian specialties are available at Goodfellows for lunch and dinner, following a morning breakfast buffet. AB, CM ($$/$$$)

GRAND HOTEL DINING ROOM

(At Grand Hotel ☎ *906.847.3331)* The Dining Room is the signature restaurant for the Grand Hotel – this is where the hotel sets the bar high. They begin the day with breakfast followed by a lunch buffet. Dinner is a five-course meal with a backdrop of chamber music. Formal dinner attire is expected for the dinner hour. Reservations are expected but not required. AB, CM, V ($$$)

HARBOR VIEW DINING

(At Chippewa Hotel ☎ 906.847.3341) Harbor View, at the Chippewa Hotel, is another signature restaurant that lives up to expectations. Dining is offered inside or outside on a garden deck. Breakfast, lunch and dinner are served. Reservations are recommended. AB, CM, V ($$$)

HORN'S GASLIGHT BAR & RESTAURANT

(Main St. ☎ 906.847.6154) Set with Western saloon-styled décor, American and Southwestern cuisine are offered for lunch, dinner and late night snacking. V, AB, CM ($$/$$$)

JOCKEY CLUB AT THE GRAND STAND

(At the Jewel Golf Course ☎ 906.847.6533) Lunch and dinner are served is style with a menu focus on sandwiches, soup and salads. Casual attire is welcome. V, AB, CM ($$/$$$)

LAKESIDE MARKET

(Mission Point Resort ☎ 906.847.3312) Hand-tossed pizza and Chicago-style hot dogs are served alongside menu offers of fruit and cheese plates, gelato and ice cream. Lakeside Market specializes in picnic lunches. Starbucks coffee is available here. V, AB, CM, NS ($)

MARTHA'S SWEET SHOP

(Main St. ☎ 906.847.3700) The aroma of fresh baked goods greets you long before you enter the shop. Open for lunch and until 3 a.m. for those midnight cravings. V, NS ($)

MARY'S BISTRO

(Next to Star Line Docks ☎ 906.847.9911) Outdoor seating and entertainment are the setting for menu items inspired by Parisian bistros. AB, CM, V ($/$$)

MIGHTY MAC HAMBURGERS

(Main St. ☎ 906.847.3307) Mighty Mac is Mackinac Island's answer to fast food. Super fast service provides better quality food than the term "fast food" usually implies. Mighty Mac offers breakfast sandwiches, hamburgers, hot dogs, chicken, fish and chili. CM ($)

MILLIE'S ON MAIN

(Main St. ☎ 906.847.3307) Millie's is a family-style restaurant serving lunch and dinner. The hearth-baked bread and Brooklyn-style pizza are especially delicious. V, CM, AB ($/$$)

MURRAY HOTEL LUNCH AND DINNER BUFFET

(Murray Hotel ☎ 906.847.8243) A delectable array of pizzas fills the lunch buffet at the Murray Hotel, and a traditional chicken dinner buffet follows for the evening meal. Both are accompanied by a 35-item salad bar. V, NS ($)

PANCAKE HOUSE

(Near Arnold Docks ☎ 906.847.3829) The Pancake House is open for breakfast and lunch serving pancakes, sandwiches, soup, ice cream and fudge. V, CM ($)

PATRICK SINCLAIR'S IRISH PUB

(Main St. ☎ 906.847.8255 ⊘ patricksinclairs.com) Corn beef sandwiches, thick chowders and their award winning Shepherd's Pie lead a menu that spans all price ranges. Live entertainment features Irish bands and karaoke. AY, AB, CM ($/$$/$$$)

PINK PONY BAR AND GRILL

(Chippewa Hotel ☎ 906.847.3341) Diners at Pink Pony can either dine inside or outside, overlooking the marina. Breakfast, lunch and dinner are served. Great Lakes fish, pasta and steaks lead the menu. Entertainment is provided as well. V, CM, AD ($$/$$$)

SEABISCUIT CAFE & GROG

(Main St. ☎ *906.847.3611)* At Seabiscuit, an international menu is well prepared and offered at a reasonable price. V, AB, CM ($$)

ROUND ISLAND BAR & GRILL

(Mission Point ☎ *906.847.3312)* Live entertainment provides the background to smoked ribs, burgers, pastas and late night snacks. Opens for lunch, dinner and evening activities. V, AB, CM ($/$$)

THREE BROTHERS SARDUCCI

(Across from Chippewa Hotel ☎ *906.847.3880)* This old-style pizzeria serves up outstanding food with fast and friendly service. Pizzas, calzones and lasagna are among the Italian specialties, and their portions are large. Open for lunch and dinner. V, CM ($)

VILLAGE INN

(Hoban St., across from Shepler's dock ☎ *906.847.3542* ⌂ *viofmackinac.com)* Recipient of the *Detroit News* "Michigan's Best" Readers Award. Open for breakfast, lunch and dinner. Their Planked Whitefish is superb. Steak, chops and ribs round out a complete menu. AY, V, AB, CM ($$/$$$)

WOODS

(Woods Golf Course, 1.5 miles from town ☎ *906.847.3699)* Woods is another Grand Hotel Restaurant. Reservations are suggested at this Bavarian-styled establishment. Live music provides a nice background for their appetizers, main courses and desserts. V, AB, CM ($$/$$$)

YANKEE REBEL TAVERN

(Astor St. ☎ *906.847.6249* ⌂ *yankeerebeltavern.com)* Yankee offers good, old-fashioned American cooking with a highlight on their Yankee pot roast and fish dishes. Chef's specials are offered daily. V, AB, CM ($$/$$$)

Did you know... ?

Mackinac Island is home to world's oldest and largest horse and buggy livery still in operation.

Mackinaw City Accommodations

Regular travelers know Mackinaw City for the quantity of rooms available. These are housed mainly in the recognizable names of several national hotel chains. This offers guests a ready familiarity with their "home away from home." The predictable format and level of service may ease some of the stress that is involved with travel plans. Scattered among these hotels are lovely bed and breakfasts, campgrounds, and intimate privately owned motels. Most types of accommodations offer free shuttle service to and from the ferry docks as well as to other places of interest in the area. Most are within easy walking distance of the downtown and shopping areas, the fort, dining, and Mackinac Island ferry services.

Seasonal rates and vacation packages are offered at most of the accommodations available. Weekends are generally priced higher than are the weekday rates. Reservations are highly recommended. At the very least, a call ahead of time to determine current rates and availability should be made.

During the off-season, Mackinac Island accommodations close, as do most (but not all) of the accommodations in Mackinaw City. Be extra vigilant about availability before your trip, if you plan on visiting during the winter.

Prices vary according to the season and day. General prices are as follows, based on average per-night rates, but prices for hotels fluctuate greatly: *$ = less than $100, $$ = $100 - $150 per night, $$$ = $150 - $200, $$$$ = $200+*. Michigan charges 6% sales tax on rooms and allows an additional 8% hotel surcharge fee.

WATERPARK HOTELS

Mackinaw City is home to several waterpark and water playground hotels. These properties are popular for families with children. The waterparks themselves are small, but they do add to the overall quality of the hotel.

AQUA GRAND MACKINAW INN AND WATERPARK

(907 S Huron Ave. ☎ *800.822.8314* ✆ *aquagrand.com)* Newly built in 2004, Aqua Grand Mackinaw Inn was updated in 2005 to include an indoor water playground and 10,000 gallon hot tub. Rooms and suites are available to accommodate any size group. Breakfast is available. ($$)

BEST WESTERN DOCKSIDE WATERFRONT

(505 S Huron St. ☎ *231.0436.5001* ✆ *bestwestern.com)* Best Western Dockside offers an indoor waterpark and pool complex, game room and exercise facilities. A quarter mile of private beach and free hot breakfast share the headline on the amenity list. Some rooms even feature heart-shaped whirlpool tubs. This resort also offers special accommodations for business with their Business Center and meeting rooms. ($$)

COMFORT SUITES LAKEVIEW

(714 S Huron Ave. ☎ *231.436.5929* ✆ *comfortsuites.com)* Comfort Suites boasts Mackinaw's largest indoor/outdoor waterpark with 75,000 gallons of water. Exercise and game rooms round out the offerings. Free hot breakfast is available. Extra large suites feature kitchens and whirlpools. Most rooms have 2 large screen televisions with VCRs. Expected amenities. ($$/$$$)

ECONO LODGE BAYVIEW

(712 S Huron St. ☎ *231.436.5777* ✆ *econolodge.com)* The park setting of 4.5 acres give this Econo Lodge a relaxing feel. Exercise and fitness rooms, game room and indoor/outdoor waterpark join indoor and outdoor pools. All rooms have refrigerators and you can select from rooms or private villas. Hot breakfast included. This is

quite a step up from the standard Econo Lodge fare. Miniature golf course and large playground are also on the property. ($$)

NORTHPOINTE INN

(1027 S Huron Ave. ☎ *231.436.9812* ✆ *northpointeinn.com)* Northpointe Inn features a new indoor waterpark, which first opened in 2008. A video game arcade, fitness room, food court and full restaurant are also on the property. Rooms vary from singles to two room and family suites. Complimentary breakfast, Internet and sandy beach access will give guests a reason to get the day started. Pricing is dependent on room type and availability. ($$/$$$)

HOTELS AND MOTELS

Mackinaw City is not known for its plush accommodations – for a true upscale experience, visitors generally prefer Mackinac Island. Nonetheless, there are a few options that offer some resort-like amenities.

The distinction between a hotel and a motel fades daily. In general, for the Mackinaw City area, motels are smaller and offer fewer perks. They are generally privately owned with lower rates. Hotels have virtually taken over the market. They have more rooms available with more courtesy accouterments. They also usually have in-house meals of some sort available. This may range from the simple continental breakfast to a full menu at an attached restaurant. Mackinaw City offers a hodgepodge of chains and smaller hotels.

AMERICA'S BEST VALUE INN

(112 Old U.S. 31 ☎ *231.436.5544* ✆ *abvimackinawcity.com)* This is one of the nicer accommodation choices available in Mackinaw City. America's Best Value Inn offers free Internet, deluxe breakfast and an indoor pool. Nice size rooms work well for families. ($)

ANCHOR BUDGET INN

(138 Old U.S. 31 ☎ *231.436.5553* ✆ *anchorbudgetinn.com)* Good service is the best recommendation for this property. They have an indoor pool and offer free tickets to Thunder Falls Waterpark, which is located across the street (details of this feature vary and should be locked in when reservations are made). The usual amenities include expanded continental breakfast. Anchor Budget Inn is open year round. ($)

BAYMONT INN & SUITES

(109 S Nicolet St. ☎ *231.436.7737* ✆ *baymontmackinaw.com)* Situated in a great location in the city and smoke free, Baymont Inn offers clean, large rooms. Lobby breakfast includes waffles, and beds feature super comfortable mattresses for a restful sleep. Expected amenities plus some extras make this a really nice place to stay. Children under 18 years old stay free. ($)

BEACHCOMBER MOTEL ON THE WATER

(1011 S Huron St. ☎ *231.436.8451)* This is a small, older facility and is well maintained, quiet and clean. Situated on Lake Huron, Beachcomber has fine views of the bridge and beach access. Bare bones amenities apply. They advertise phones and a playground as customer drawing features. ($)

THE BEACH HOUSE

(11490 U.S. 23 ☎ *231.436.5353* ✆ *beachhouse@mackinawcity.com)* Cottages on the Straits of Mackinac, Lake Huron side, have a retro '70/80s feel. Nice, sandy beachfront and indoor pool are features of this facility. A limited number of kitchenettes give guests more options for meals. Homemade muffins and coffee help visitors greet the day. Dogs are welcome upon approval. ($)

BEST WESTERN THUNDERBIRD INN

(146 Old U.S. 31 ☎ *231.436.5433* ⌂ *bestwesternthunderbirdinn.com)* A comfortable, predictable place to use as home base for a vacation, Best Western Thunderbird is a nice, clean place with no surprises. It offers all the standard Best Western amenities as well as an indoor pool. A deluxe breakfast is also included. ($)

BUDGET HOST AMERICAN BOUTIQUE INN

(517 N Huron Ave. ☎ *231.436.5543* ⌂ *americanboutiqueinns.com)* "Boutique" is the key word here. Rooms are small and were individually theme-decorated some years ago. They have received *Budget Host's* 4 Lantern "Award of Excellence" for 8 years. They offer an outdoor pool and personalized service. Recommended for couples and singles. ($)

CLARION HOTEL BEACHFRONT

(905 S Huron Ave. ☎ *231.436.5539* ⌂ *mackinawreservations.com/clarion)* An indoor pool and an outdoor pool offer the best of both worlds. This Clarion is geared for families and groups on vacation. They offer nightly campfires on the beach and free breakfasts. "Family Fun Rooms" are suites that feature bunk beds for the kids in a room separate from the parents and full kitchens. Price varies according to room style and location. ($/$$)

COMFORT INN - LAKESIDE

(611 S Huron Ave. ☎ *231.436.5057* ⌂ *comfortinnmackinaw.com)* Winner of the *2007 Choice Platinum Hospitality Award*, they offer unlimited access to the indoor/outdoor waterpark at the neighboring hotel in addition to their own indoor pool. Other features include a nice beachfront and deluxe continental breakfast. This Comfort Inn is located close to the ferries to Mackinac Island. ($$)

COURTYARD INN & SUITES OF MACKINAW

(202 E Central Ave. ☎ 231.436.5528 ⌐ courtyardinnmackinaw.com)
The Courtyard Inn is unbelievably immaculate and the continental breakfast is hosted in a courtyard setting. Indoor pool and outdoor playground offer distractions after a busy day. Typical amenities supplied with good service. ($$)

DAYS INN LAKEVIEW

(825 S Huron St. ☎ 231.436.5557 ⌐ daysinnlakeview.com) The Days Inn Lakeview features clean rooms, an indoor pool and whirlpool. Typical Days Inn standards make it comfortable and predictable. ($)

DAYS INN & SUITES BRIDGEVIEW LODGE

(206 N Nicolet St. ☎ 231.436.8961) The honeymoon suite with hot tub and private balcony is a nice break from the other more family oriented suites consisting of 2 or 3 rooms. Standard rooms are also available. Indoor pool and hot breakfast are included with accommodations. Standard amenities are available. ($)

ECONO LODGE – AT THE BRIDGE

(412 N Nicolet St. ☎ 231.436.5026 ⌐ econolodge.com/hotel/MI098)
Good location with basic amenities. Although there is no pool, no king size beds or suites, the place is neat and inviting. All room doors also open to parking. Open all year, AAA discounts offered. ($)

FLAMINGO MOTEL

(13959 Mackinaw Hwy ☎ 231.436.751 ⌐ mackinaw-city-motel.com)
The Flamingo is located two miles south of town. It is a nice, quiet location that welcomes small pets. While beautifully maintained, it is an economy motel offering the basics. It is open year round and

offers the easiest access to snowmobile trails of all the accommodations available. ($)

GRAND VIEW RESORT – BEACHFRONT

(1143 S Huron Ave. ☎ *231.436.8100)* Grand View is simple and straightforward. It is a nice, clean place to stay. Indoor and outdoor pools are available in addition to 230 feet of beach access. Free hot breakfasts start the day and nightly beach campfires close the day out. ($)

GREAT LAKES INN

(900 S Huron Ave. ☎ *231.436.7900)* A new name for an old favorite, this facility is clean and nicely maintained. Great Lakes Inn features the standard amenities (without the breakfast) and has two pools on site; one indoor and one outdoor with sundeck. A special sprinkler park will have the kids giggling in no time. Jacuzzi king suites are offered for the grown ups. ($)

HAMILTON INN SELECT BEACHFRONT

(701 S Huron Ave. ☎ *231.436.5005)* Hamilton Inn offers breakfast, pool, beach access, and standard amenities. They are open all year with some rooms featuring private whirlpool tubs. ($)

HAMPTON INN

(726 S Huron Ave. ☎ *231.436.7829)* Hampton Inn features very nice non-smoking rooms (on a non-smoking floor) along with an indoor pool, complimentary hot breakfast and Internet access. The real secret to this one is the mattresses: Cloud 9 beds and carpet – this means extra comfy and welcoming. ($)

HOLIDAY INN EXPRESS - "AT THE BRIDGE"

(364 Louvigny ☎ *231.436.7100* ✆ *expressmackinaw.com)* This Holiday Inn Express offers a complimentary hot breakfast to each guest with cinnamon rolls and omelets leading a buffet of choices. A fit-

ness room, spa and indoor pool top the list of amenities. The "Mackinaw Club Level" hosts two room deluxe suites. "Deluxe" refers to the wet bars, fireplaces, Jacuzzi tubs and private balconies that are standard on this level. ($$)

PARKSIDE INN – BRIDGEVIEW

(771 N Huron Ave. ☎ *231.436.8301* ⌁ *parksideinn.com)* Parkside is a nice place to stay with all the things that are expected in a quality hotel, including: an indoor pool, beach access, free hot breakfast, fitness and game rooms. ($$)

QUALITY INN & SUITES BEACHFRONT

(917 S Huron Dr. ☎ *231.436.5051* ⌁ *qualityinn.com)* On the first floor of this Quality Inn, rooms have private access to the beach, while the upper floors feature balconies that overlook the waterfront. A lovely, new garden breakfast room hosts complimentary hot breakfasts every morning. Standard amenities apply, including an indoor pool. ($$)

RAMADA INN WATERFRONT

(723 S Huron Ave. ☎ *231.436.5055* ⌁ *ramada.com)* Suites with and without hot tubs are available while every room has a balcony, refrigerator and microwave. The indoor pool and whirlpool are joined by an outdoor rooftop whirlpool and sundeck. A honeymoon suite for romantics is also offered. Expect the standard amenities, which includes free breakfast. ($$)

RIVIERA MOTEL

(520 N Huron Ave. ☎ *231.436.5577* ⌁ *shadowofthebridge.com)* The Riviera Motel offers the basic amenities with an outdoor pool and beach access. It is the closest accommodation to the bridge and excels in straightforward service. A good place to stay. ($)

SUPER 8 MOTEL BEACHFRONT

(519 S Huron St. ☎ *231.436.7111* ⟨ᵗ⟩ *super8.com)* The Super 8 Beachfront is a nice facility, but nothing outstanding sets it apart. It meets all the standard requirements of a nice hotel: hot breakfast, indoor pool, and non-smoking rooms. ($$)

SUPER 8 MOTEL BRIDGEVIEW

(601 N Huron Ave. ☎ *231.436.5252* ⟨ᵗ⟩ *super8.com)* This natural log cabin-style property offers slightly more amenities than the Beachfront Super 8 along with complimentary breakfast, indoor pool and beach access via the state park. They also have Jacuzzi suites available. ($$)

BED AND BREAKFASTS

Bed and Breakfasts are privately owned residences that offer sleeping quarters and breakfasts to their guests. The hosts are ready to assist the traveler in a myriad of friendly ways. Other meals are occasionally offered for additional charges. These accommodations are frequently custom decorated, inviting the visitor to relax in style. Prices vary widely as does availability.

BRIGADOON BED AND BREAKFAST

(207 Langlade St. ☎ *231.436.8882* ⟨ᵗ⟩ *mackinawbrigadoon.com)* The Brigadoon is situated just behind the main street under some gorgeous, large trees. The Victorian-styled home is smoke free with eight guest suites that each include a balcony, fireplace, and king-size canopy bed. It offers a quiet refuge while still being within easy walking distance of main attractions. Adults are the preferred clientele. This is easily the most elegant place to stay in Mackinaw City. ($$/$$$)

DEERHEAD INN BED & BREAKFAST

(109 Henry St. ☎ *231.436.3337)* Slightly farther off of the beaten path, this smaller facility is furnished in an inviting classic "up north" fashion. The house is an "arts and crafts"-style home from the turn of the last century and is truly fun to see. The owners are history buffs and have fascinating true stories to share of life in early Mackinaw. They respect the privacy of their guests and feature full breakfasts. Fireplaces and unique décor grace each bedroom. Open year round. ($)

CAMPGROUNDS

Overnight camping is not allowed on Mackinac Island, so those who want to sleep in the Great Outdoors will have to choose a campground on the mainland. The Mackinaw City are has a few nearby campgrounds, but northern Michigan is filled with many places to camp for those willing to drive a bit.

MACKINAW CITY/MACKINAC ISLAND KOA

(566 Trailsend Rd. ☎ *231.436.5643* ⏚ *koa.com)* Located on the west side of Mackinaw City, this KOA offers free shuttle rides to the ferry docks. The owners are locals who look for ways to assist their guests in enjoying their stay. Sites are shaded and level, some with concrete surfacing. Amenities include a heated pool, pull thru sites, evening movies, nature trails, and full sewer hookups. ($)

TEE PEE CAMPGROUND

(11262 W. U.S. 23 ☎ *231.436.5391* ⏚ *tee-peecampgrounds.com)* The campground is situated east of Mackinaw City on the shores of Lake Huron. Bonfires are hosted on the shore each evening along with other activities. Sites are more uneven and seem smaller than those at the KOA campground. Since they host fewer sites, this would make them a nice group camping experience. Standard

amenities are included as well as a shuttle to the ferries. Their web-site redirects to a national search which can be confusing, so calling them is probably preferred. The hosts are longtime residents and enjoy sharing their hospitality. ($)

Mackinac Island Accommodations

Mackinac Island is home to the glamorous side of the Mackinac area. This lovely isle, where voyageurs and natives once roughed it in makeshift camps, has been transformed into the gold standard of hospitality. The island has a permanent home for the Governor of the State of Michigan and routinely hosts leaders from across the globe. Celebrities from the diverse worlds of cinema, theater, sports, literature, science and many others all seek the unique refuge of Mackinac Island. It has even served as the setting for romantic movies: *This Time for Keeps*, (1949) starring Esther Williams, and *Somewhere in Time* (1980) starring Jane Seymour and Christopher Reeve.

Most hotels on Mackinac Island have a strict "no pets" policy (except for service animals). All accommodations are open May through October unless noted otherwise.

Prices are more expensive on Mackinac Island than in Mackinaw City. Average prices here are based on a one-night stay: *$ = less than $100, $$ = $200-$400, $$$ = $500-$700, $$$$ = more than $700.* Exact pricing should always be verified at the time of reservation.

RESORTS

Mackinac Island's few resorts represent a gold standard for the hospitality industry. They combine the modern conveniences of full-service hotels with a kind of classical grace found in few other places in America. Visitors arrive not by taxi, but by horse and carriage. Urban congestion is replaced by a relaxed, spacious atmosphere. Of course, all this comes with a cost, so be prepared to pay for these luxuries.

GRAND HOTEL 🈲

(1 Grand St. ☎ *906.847.3331* ✆ *grandhotel.com)* The Grand Hotel is the finest hotel in Michigan. Sometimes referred to as "The Grand," this is the most famous spot in the Mackinac area. Built in 1887 to meet the needs of the changing island clientele, its late-19th-century architecture is a classic beauty. The hotel has been visited by Thomas Edison, Mark Twain, five U.S. presidents, and countless celebrities. It is also a designated National Historic Landmark. The Grand is the winner of awards too numerous to list here (for example, it is one of *Travel & Leisure's* "Best Hotels in the World"). This is the epitome of Mackinac and well worth investigating, even if you don't plan on spending the night.

Everything here is done on a "grand" scale. From the exquisite gardens and golfing facilities to the detailed attention in service, they strive to please. Their purebred horses and authentic livery appointments are among the best in the world; a beautiful sight to see (the stables are open to the public). Their facility is home to clothing boutiques, confections, restaurants and much, much more. One of The Grand's trademark amenities it its long **front porch** which, at about 660 feet, is claimed to be the longest in the world. The porch is lined with rocking chairs and is a favorite place for guests to sit and relax.

The hotel's **Main Dining Room** serves complimentary breakfast and dinner for all hotel guests, and you'll be hard-pressed to find better food in all of Mackinac. During the dinner hour, eveningwear (suit and tie for men, dress or pantsuit for women) is required in all public areas of the hotel.

Despite its upscale appearance, The Grand is also one of the most family-friendly hotels in America, and has been given top ratings to this effect. Children 11 years old and under stay and eat at no cost, and reduced rates are offered for those 17 years old and under. There are numerous children's programs scheduled throughout the summer, not to mention its location on kid-friendly Mackinac Island.

The resort-quality **Esther Williams outdoor pool** is free for hotels guest, and open to visitors for a fee. This allows day use of the pool and the surrounding area, which includes play areas, game courts, lunch and snack bars. The pool is an outdoor facility nestled in the midst of a luxurious garden setting. ($$/$$$)

MISSION POINT RESORT

(1 Lakeshore Dr. ☎ *800.833.7711 for reservations/906.847.3312 for hotel direct* ☝ *missionpoint.com)* Nestled in a quiet corner of the island is the campus of Mission Point Resort. Built on the location of the first Protestant mission (thus the name) established in the Mackinac area, it boasts a fascinating history and has an atmosphere of casual refinement. Soaring log architecture hearkens back to the roots of the island while offering the best of hospitality.

Four restaurants bring an array of dining experiences for the guest. Large events such as conferences and weddings are welcome. An 18-hole putting course with real bent grass greens, bike rentals, theater and a 3,000-square-foot supervised children's activity center are among the many outstanding features of this facility. Lots to do here without leaving the grounds. A 10-minute walk gives easy access into the main downtown area. ($$/$$$)

HOTELS AND MOTELS

Even the most basic accommodations on Mackinac Island seem to outdo their mainland contenders.

CHIPPEWA HOTEL WATERFRONT

(Main St. ☎ *800.241.3341* ☝ *chippewahotel.com)* Located on the waterfront in downtown Mackinac Island, this hotel is right in the center of the action. Street side rooms and suites are available at lower rates than the waterfront accommodations. Numerous specials and packages help create the perfect vacation. Amenities begin

with the standard Internet, cable television, and queen size bed before soaring with the addition of services that may include nightly
turn down service with milk and cookies, in room Jacuzzi, pillow
top mattress, and four-poster king size bed. ($$ - $$$)

HARBOUR VIEW INN

(P.O. Box 1207 ☎ *906.847.0101* ✆ *harbourviewinn.com)* This property was originally built in 1820 as the finest home on the island for
the queen of the fur trade, Madame LaFramboise. Today the home
has been upgraded to contain 82 guest rooms and suites. The décor
blends French and Victorian styles. A complimentary deluxe break-
fast leads the list of expected amenities. ($$)

HOTEL IROQUOIS

(7485 Main St. ☎ *906.847.3321 for April-October/616.247.5675 for
November-March* ✆ *iroquoishotel.com)* The Iroquois is part of the *Condé
Nast* "Gold List," which praises uniqueness and service of its
properties. The cottage décor and discreet placement of edifices on
the property give the ambiance of peaceful solitude while being
located a shy block from town. Complimentary movies are avail-
able from the front desk. Suites feature a wet bar and whirlpool
tubs. As a non-smoking and non-pet historic hotel, the amenities
are of the high quality expected on the island. The private beach
and upscale restaurant on-site create a complete vacation spot.
Children are welcome but the hotel is designed as an upscale geta-
way for adults. ($$/$$$$)

ISLAND HOUSE HOTEL

(P.O. Box 1410 ☎ *906.847.3347* ✆ *theislandhouse.com)* The Island
House Hotel is a State of Michigan Landmark and is registered
with the Historic Hotels of America National Trust for Historic
Preservation. This beautiful hotel has been in business for 150
years, with the distinction of being the first summer hotel on the
island. As the only hotel located within the Mackinac Island State

Park, vistas from the hotel include Lake Huron and lovely wooded bluffs. Renovations in 2008 completely upgraded amenities in all parts of the facility and made the property as eco-friendly as possible. Smoking is only allowed in designated areas to keep the rooms smoke free. Renovations paid special attention to creating a barrier free and handicap accessible environment.

Amenities include a wonderful Pool House that features an indoor pool, sauna, spa and sundeck. Complimentary bikes allow guests to explore the trails throughout the island. Room rates are classified as "Bed & Breakfast" where rates include breakfast, "Modified American" that include breakfast and dinner and "European" consisting of rooms only, no meals. Their **1852 Grill Room** is highly acclaimed. ($$/$$$)

LAKE VIEW HOTEL
(1 Huron St. ☎ *906.847.3384* ⏏ *lake-view-hotel.us)* Conference and banquet rooms join two restaurants and three specialty shops in giving this hotel a resort atmosphere. Its location on Main Street encloses an indoor pool. The owners have created a barrier free environment that includes an elevator. There are no pets, no balconies, and no smoking. Children 16 years old and under stay free when staying in the same rooms the parents. This is a very nice vacation option. ($/$$)

LILAC TREE HOTEL AND SPA
(Main St. ☎ *906.847.6575* ⏏ *lilactree.com)* This pretty hotel is a sister hotel to the Chippewa. It features the most updated banquet room and dance floor. Lilac Tree looks to specialize in weddings and other group events. All suites are non-smoking and include refrigerators, microwaves, televisions and nightly bed turndowns. Children 17 years and under stay free with the parents. Reservations require a two-night minimum stay during weekends. ($/$$)

MAIN STREET INN AND SUITES

(Main St. ☎ *906.847.6530* ⌖ *mainstreetinnandsuites.com)* Pillow-top mattresses adorn the king and queen size beds available in the suites and deluxe rooms offered at Main Street Inn. All suites feature balconies overlooking Main Street. Hanging flower baskets create a garden ambiance in the middle of the city and immediately catch the eye. The interior is even more gracious. Far from being noisy with street sounds, these rooms were constructed with sound buffers that turn guest quarters into a peaceful retreat. It is a non-smoking, barrier-free facility. Two honeymoon suites are featured. They include hot tubs, wet bar, two television sets and terry cloth robes. Children 17 years and under stay for no charge. There is a two-night minimum for weekends throughout September and October. ($/$$)

MURRAY HOTEL

(Main St. ☎ *800-4-MACKINAC* ⌖ *4mackinac.com)* Affordable luxury is the motto at the Murray Hotel, and it is an accurate one. Home-baked "bedtime cookies" top off a fun day spent at the outdoor spa and pool or exploring the island. Complimentary deluxe breakfast bar, nightly movies, conference room and banquet facilities give this facility a well-rounded offering to guests. An onsite deli and café specializes in great pizza. Murray Hotel is a smoke-free establishment. ($/$$)

THE INN AT STONECLIFFE

(West Bluff ☎ *906.847.3355* ⌖ *theinnatstonecliffe.com)* Built as a one-of-a-kind summer estate, The Inn at Stonecliffe has recently been restored to its original beauty, inside and out. It is the farthest from the heavily traveled tourist areas while being the closet to the airport. It is a nice bicycle or carriage ride into the main areas of the island. The property features the original house with guest rooms that are smoke free, television free and the perfect tranquil environment. Additional buildings present guests options that range

from studio-style suites to more modern décor that includes televisions. Exquisite gardens provide the backdrop for outdoor weddings and gatherings. A professional wedding planner is on staff. Unique and lovely reception facilities are also available. A pool and an award-winning gourmet restaurant are onsite. The full hot breakfast is complimentary. ($/$$)

WINDERMERE HOTEL

(Main St. ☎ *906.847.3301* ⌁ *windermerehotel.com)* The Windermere is another summer-residence-turned-hotel. For more than 100 years, the Doud family has offered hospitality to island guests. They keep things simple and true to the heritage of the home with a basic continental breakfast, no televisions in the rooms, no in room telephones and no hotel surcharge. The décor brings a turn of the last century charm that is irresistible. Children under 16 years old stay free. This is a beautiful place to come and enjoy. ($$)

BED AND BREAKFASTS

Mackinac Island's Bed and Breakfasts offer a quaint and often romantic alternative to the larger resorts and hotels on the island.

BAY COTTAGE

(☎ *906.847.3401* ⌁ *mackinac.com/baycottage)* This 1825 Federal Colonial-style home is available for weekly rental. The master suite has a private bath, as does one other suite in the home. Two additional bedrooms share a full bath. A cleverly remodeled carriage house features a living room, kitchen, two bedrooms and one full bath. Fees are determined according the number of persons in the registering party and the season. They are open year round. ($$$$)

BAY VIEW AT MACKINAC

(☎ 906.847.3295 ☞ mackinacbayview.com) Private baths accompany each room at Bay View. This is a non-smoking home with wireless Internet and reception facilities. They offer a complimentary after-noon tea and evening dessert in addition to the breakfast. ($/$$)

CHATEAU LORRAINE AND PINE COTTAGE

(☎ 906.847.3820 ☞ mackinac.com/pinecottage) Breakfast is served on silver and china. Homemade breads and breakfast cakes are served daily. Pine Cottage has a more rustic décor than Chateau Lorraine, but the same friendliness. Both feature rooms with private or semi-private baths. Rooms are available from May through September. ($/$$)

CLOGHAUN BED AND BREAKFAST

(Market St. ☎ 906.847.3885 ☞ cloghaun.com) Smoking is allowed only on the porch. Out of consideration for the variety of guests that are hosted, children over two years old are welcome only if they are strictly supervised. Pets are not accommodated. A deli-cious complimentary afternoon tea joins the complimentary deluxe breakfast. ($ /$$)

COTTAGE INN OF MACKINAC

(Market St. ☎ 906.847.4000 ☞ cottageinnofmackinac.com) Private baths join each room of this non-smoking inn. Pillow-top beds and a deluxe breakfast show the owners desire to make this a welcom-ing place. Complimentary coffee and beverages are available all day, culminating with afternoon tea with homemade treats. ($ /$$)

MARKET STREET INN

(Market St. ☎ 888.899.3811 ☞ mackinac.com/marketstreetinn) Feather beds, private baths, and wireless Internet await guests at the inn. Two king-size Jacuzzi suites are outstanding features. ($/$$)

Did you know… ?

The Grand Hotel claims to have the world's longest porch.

Day Trips

From the convenience of Mackinaw City and Mackinac Island, a mere 90 minute drive north, south, east or west opens up new venues to explore. With central accommodations in Mackinaw City or on Mackinac Island, these regions may be sampled.

North of the Mackinac Bridge is the Upper Peninsula of Michigan. Touching three of the Great Lakes, this peninsula has developed a unique cultural heritage. The people here have intertwined to form a closely-knit community that relishes their status as "yoopers" (Pronounced "you-pers"). This is not a highly urbanized area, even in the cities. The pace of life is unhurried. It takes a hardy, practical perspective on life to survive the rugged challenges that nature routinely throws over this peninsula. Harsh winters are the price that is paid for choosing to live in the wildly beautiful North Country. A tough pride has developed concerning their history, future and neighborliness.

The Upper Peninsula became the concourse of Native American and European nations before the Lower Peninsula did. Jesuit Missions at Sault Ste. Marie and St. Ignace are the first European establishments in Michigan. Naturally, the Native Americans had established communities in these locations long before the Europeans ever crossed the ocean. Father Marquette moved his original mission on Mackinac Island to St. Ignace because of this factor. These two towns are within a one hour drive of Mackinaw City. The area west of St. Ignace, on U.S. 2, is full of potential for modern explorers.

SAULT STE. MARIE

Situated on the northern shore of the peninsula, where Lake Superior rushes and falls into the St. Marys River, is Sault Sainte Marie, the oldest city in Michigan. The local Chippewa community referred to the area as "bawating" meaning the "gathering place" with a particular reference to the excellent fishing on with the tribe depended. The voyageurs who frequented the waters here called it "Sault du Gascogne." Gascogne or Gascony is a region in southwest France known for its challenging waterways. The word, "sault" is an old French word for "jump." That is a very apt description of the rapids. Voyageurs found it necessary to portage their boats and goods around the wide rapids. Father Marquette and Claude Dablon established a mission in 1668. Father Marquette renamed the spot as Sault Ste. Marie after the Virgin Mary. It is pronounced as "soo (sue)" and not the common mispronunciation of "salt." Many refer to it simply as "the Soo." This nickname heralds from the earliest French influences at these rapids. The locals are always pleased to hear their home referred to correctly.

Sault Ste. Marie actually grew up on both sides of the rapids. It became divided due to politics. The north shore is home to Sault Ste. Marie, Ontario, Canada. Industry is the main stay of this community. They have an indoor mall for shopping and a developing array of tourist attractions. The two cities, countries actually, are joined by the International Bridge. A train trestle runs parallel to the bridge. It rises when necessary to accommodate passage of the largest freighters.

The tourist boom that occurred with the opening of the Mackinac Bridge brought a profusion of the dreaded tourist traps to Sault Ste. Marie, MI. Most of these have faded into the past. The Strip, as locals call Portage Avenue, is home to the prerequisite fudge shops and gift stores. The merchandise offered is superior to the overpriced, plastic souvenirs of the past. Replacing the faddish traps are quality museums and exhibits. Lake Superior State University joins theater groups downtown to add classic cultural events to the venue of things to do in the Soo. Their sports teams are showcased in competitive events open to the public. Ice hockey dominates in the role usually held by university football.

Here are some of the best attractions that Sault Ste. Marie has to offer. Most of these have been a long time in planning and it is with great pride that they are open to guests.

THE SOO LOCKS

This engineering marvel is more than 150 years old. Frustration over the impediment to trade caused by the rapids and twenty foot drop from Lake Superior to the St. Mary's River produced the first wooden lock to be built in 1797. It was destroyed in the War of 1812. New locks were opened for business on May 31, 1855. Continual upgrades keep the Locks current to the needs of modern shipping. They are the busiest locks in the world and the largest in the western hemisphere.

The **Visitors Center**, (☎ *906.253.9101* ⌁ *soolocksvisitorscenter.com)* located in the midst of a beautiful park and gardens, features displays and a free movie that explains how the locks work and their history. The staff here is wonderful, full of helpful information and suggestions. Vessel arrival information is available at the front desk. It is best to stop here and become familiarized with the locks prior to actually going out to see them.

The park is home of several artifacts donated to the city throughout the years. Observation platforms line the fence that separates the park from the mooring area. These provide uninhibited viewing of the freighters as they negotiate the locks. The viewing could not be any closer unless visitors volunteer for ship duty. A handicap accessible viewing area is also available by permission at the eastern end of the locks. Staff members at the Visitors Center are happy to assist with this service. Weekly concerts in the park are performed at no charge throughout the summer months. Entrance to the park is free. Contact the Visitors Center for up to the minute information.

SOO LOCKS BOAT TOURS

(1157 Portage Ave. (Dock #1)/515 Portage Avenue (Dock #2)
☎ *906.632.6301 ⌁ soolocks.com)* Visitors are invited to experience firsthand the drama of "locking through" the world famous Soo Locks. The boat tour continues with a sightseeing excursion of waterfront history along Michigan and Canadian shorelines. Tour is approximately two hours in length. The cruise boats are climate controlled for comfort. An on-board snack bar sells refreshments. Additional cruise choices include a dinner cruise and St. Marys River cruise. Groups are welcome and custom excursions are offered. Free kennel service is available for tour boat clients. Docks and boats are handicap accessible. Passports are not required to participate on this excursion. Adults fare is $21.00 (U.S.), children 5-12 years at $10.50 (U.S.), those 4 years and under ride free. They operate May to Mid-October, rain or shine, seven days a week.

MAHDEZEWIN INTERNATIONAL

(807 Ashmun St. ☎ 906.635.8227) Their named is derived from the Chippewa word meaning "essence of existence." They have set the goal of building a bridge of understanding concerning the past, present and future of the Original People to the area. A Woodland Cultural Resource Center brings presentations, workshops and additional learning opportunities to the public for nominal fees. They present Native American arts and crafts for purchase. Hours are noon until 6:00 p.m., 6 days a week.

OFFICIAL SURVEY MONUMENT OF MICHIGAN

Each state has a set of base survey lines from which all property surveys are articulated. Sault Ste. Marie is the northern terminus of the Prime Meridian for Michigan. The southern point is in Defiance, Ohio. This termination point is located by the rail bridge, near the International Bridge. The line was fixed in 1815 with the east-west line running from Detroit to Lake Michigan. The official survey of Michigan's Lower Peninsula was completed in 1840. The Upper Peninsula survey was complete in 1851.

RIVER OF HISTORY MUSEUM

(209 E. Portage Ave. ☎ *888.744.7867* ⌇ *saulthistoricsites.com)* Eleven galleries tell the tale of Native American, French, British and American life on the St. Mary's River in chronological order. This is a new museum that has been in the planning for a long time so it is exciting to see it ready for guests. Well-done displays are accompanied by audio narration. Rates are $6.00 for adults and $3.00 for children ages 6 to 17 years. A discount is given with a combined ticket purchase that includes the Museum Boat Valley Camp and the Tower of History. Open May through October.

TOWER OF HISTORY

(501 E Water St. ☎ *906.632.3658* ⌇ *saulthistoricsites.com)* Soaring 210 feet high, the view from the tower is spectacular. In addition to an overview of the locks and immediate surroundings, it is possible to see 1,200 square miles that include the St. Mary's River and untouched Canadian Wilderness. Displays assist in locating landmarks and tell of area origins. An express elevator transports guests to this bird's eye view. Bring a camera! Rates for adults are $6.50, children ages 6- 17 years are $3.25. A discount is available when purchased in combination with the Museum Boat Valley Camp and River of History Museum tickets. Open May through October, 10 a.m. -5:00 p.m. daily.

MUSEUM SHIP VALLEY CAMP

(501 E Water St. ☎ *906.632.3658* ⌇ *saulthistoricsites.com)* Maritime history comes alive on the 550 ft long Valley Camp. Built in 1917, the ship plied the Great Lakes with her 32-man crew until her retirement in 1968. She reached her final mooring in time for the tricentennial of the founding of Sault Ste. Marie. Visitors are invited to explore every nook and cranny of the ship, including the Cap-

tain's quarters. Four 1,200 gallon aquariums showcase fish species of the Great Lakes. Displays and exhibits give permanent homes to maritime artifacts. This museum is packed with items to see and experience. Quarters can be a bit tight, as necessitated for life on board ship. Not recommended for strollers or wheelchairs. Please wear soft soles when on board. Open daily from mid-May through mid-October. Adult rates are $6.50 (U.S.), children 6-17 years for $3.25 (U.S.). A discount is available when purchased in combination with the Tower of History and River of History Museum tickets.

WATER STREET HISTORIC BLOCK

(501 E Water St. ☎ *906.632.3658* ✆ *saulthistoricsites.com)* The site is a historically accurate portrayal of the homes and lives of early residents of the Soo. The Johnston House has original family artifacts of John Johnston, one of the first full time European residents. The office of Indian Agent Henry Schoolcraft has been reconstructed to reflect the importance of relations in the area. Local performers and artisans bring the exhibits living color. The Kemp Coal Office has a museum as well. It details the industrial history of Sault Ste. Marie. Open daily from mid-May through mid-October. Adult rates are $6.00 (U.S.), children 6-17 years for $3.00 (U.S.).

ST. IGNACE

Father Marquette noticed the large population of natives at the southern edge of the Upper Peninsula, the northern side of the Straits of Mackinac. He concluded that his mission would reach more people if he joined them. In 1671, he permanently moved his mission here. He named it Saint Ignace after the founder of the Jesuits, St. Ignatius Loyola. This would become the spot that he considered home for the remainder of his life. His explorations took him as far as the Mississippi River. Sadly, he died of illness on his return trip, all the while longing for his St. Ignace home.

As the fur trade grew, the natural harbor at St. Ignace made the Upper Peninsula more accessible than the lands on the south side of the straits. As a result, the Lower Peninsula lay dormant to European exploration for a number of years.

The fur trade was replaced by logging and commercial fishing. These industries relied heavily on this harbor for their success. St. Ignace grew in importance and the county seat was moved here from Mackinac Island. It remained as one of the largest fishing ports of the Great Lakes until the opening of the Mackinac Bridge. With the bridge opening, St. Ignace looked for a new way to sustain itself. Tourism began as travelers flocked to the area in search of relief from respiratory ailments.

This is a quiet, friendly town. The residents here value community, family and friendships more than showy, ostentatious displays. Tucked throughout their town are historical markers and displays so a walking tour of town is encouraged. Locals look forward to meeting guests of their town and sharing the highlights.

Just outside of the formal downtown area are several noteworthy sites. They are given here and recommended for every visitor to the straits.

FATHER MARQUETTE NATIONAL MEMORIAL
(Inside Straits State Park, West of I-75 on U.S. 2 ☎ 906.643.6627)
Proudly overlooking the straits stands the Father Marquette Memorial. A 15 station outdoor interpretive walk details life here as Father Marquette knew it. The park also offers picnic sites, hiking trails and camping. A State Park vehicle pass is needed to gain entrance and may be purchased on site. Open from Memorial Day through Labor Day weekend. Pets are allowed on a leash. The site is handicap accessible. Guests are encouraged to allow one hour for the interpretive walk.

FORT DE BUADE MUSEUM

(☎ 906.643.6627 ◌ fortdebuade.bravehost.com) As the largest museum in Michigan, artifacts from pre-European contact to modern times are on display. A movie, with free popcorn, helps to explain the intricacies of the past. It is very unimposing on the exterior, looking similar to an old fashioned tourist trap. Don't be deceived! This is an excellent, must see place. It began as a private collection of artifacts, antiques and relics that spanned fifty years. The 5,000 piece collection and building (a former warehouse) was purchased by the City of St. Ignace with the help of the Chippewa Tribe. It is open to visitors free of charge. Open daily from May through October. They have a helpful website, but the host site does not direct to it. It works best if it is located through a search engine. Hopefully they will fix this.

CASTLE ROCK

(☎ 906.643.8268) Visible in the west, long before the connecting exit off of I-75, is a tall natural rock formation. It resembles the tower of a medieval castle. At its base sits Paul Bunyan, the giant logger of folklore and his blue ox, Babe. A wooden staircase leads climbers to the top and a view that is unsurpassed. There are resting spots on the way up but this is not a climb for the frail. A large souvenir and gift shop sells the tickets needed to gain entrance to the staircase. One ticket is 50 cents: half of a dollar. The price holds for everyone. They are open seven days a week, May through October. To get there, use exit 348 off of I-75.

GREAT LAKES AIR, INC.

(☎ 906.643.7165) Great Lakes Air flies out of the Mackinac County Airport daily. The experienced pilots normally ferry people and goods to and from Mackinac Island. They also enjoy giving tour rides over the straits and do a fantastic job of pointing out landmarks and just generally creating an informative, exciting ride for their guests. Cameras are welcome. Pricing varies but is reason-

able. They are just off of the I-75 Business Loop exiting east on the north end of St. Ignace.

EASTERN UPPER PENINSULA FISHING CHARTERS

(W770 Cheeseman Rd. ☎ *877.475.3474* ✆ *eupfishingcharters.com)* They catch fish on every excursion into the waters between St. Ignace and Mackinac Island. All equipment is furnished and kept in the best condition. They are fully licensed and insured. This is a prime way to find out first hand if the claim of great fishing at the straits is accurate. Forty years of experience in the figure of the Captain will be at your service. Rates flex between $250 and $500. The website accommodates many fishing and hunting services.

DREAM SEAKER CHARTERS AND TOURS

(P.O. Box 282, Pickford, MI ☎ *906.647.7276* ✆ *dreamseaker.com)* Misspelling the word "seeker" for marketing purposes, this company charters their services for a half or a fully day of family fishing or just cruising around the Les Cheneaux Islands with a "No skunk" guarantee. Rates for fishing charters begin at $450 for 1-4 people. Island tours vary in length from one hour up to three hours. The price range begins at $225 for 1-4 persons. They are located on the far eastern shore of the Upper Peninsula between St. Ignace and Sault Ste. Marie.

NORTHERN LAKE MICHIGAN

On the southern shore of the Upper Peninsula lies Lake Michigan. Many tiny villages dot this shore in remembrance to the logging industry that once shipped from their ports. Restaurants are few and far between. It is best to eat before leaving the St. Ignace area or to pack a picnic. Roadside parks offer picnicking facilities and other necessary conveniences. Some of these parks are situated next to rivers and waterfalls or excellent vantage points for viewing

Lake Michigan and the numerous small islands near the banks. Take the U.S. 2 west highway exit off of I-75, just across the Mackinac Bridge, for access to the attractions recommended.

As soon as the bridge is crossed, billboards will grab your attention, advertising the "world famous" **Mystery Spot**, an attraction that has been around for a very long time. It is one of the original tourist spots and many refer to it as a tourist trap. It is not a recommended stop. The little children may be amused but the price is rather steep for a few moments of suspended logic.

LAKE MICHIGAN SAND DUNES

Sand, sand, sand! Everywhere! This sandy shore is one of the absolutely best places for a day at the beach. The white, soft sand leads water lovers into shallow waters warmed by the sun. The water is clear and sparkles. It has an extensive shallow area before reaching deeper depths for more experienced swimmers. No lifeguards are ever on duty so play in the water at your own risk. It is one of the best beaches in Michigan. The sand dunes also feature hiking and cross country ski trails sponsored by the State of Michigan.

STRAITS UNDERWATER DIVE PRESERVE

(☎ *906.643.8718* ✆ *michiganpreserves.org)* For those who dive, this is one of the best experiences around. Rock formations and shipwrecks in the straits are marked for convenience.

WEIRD MICHIGAN WAX MUSEUM

(On U.S. 2 at Martin Lake Rd. ☎ *906.643.8760* ✆ *weirdwax.com)* It may sound a little strange and that is what they hope guests will find. Strange figures lurk in the museum, bringing legends, folklore and weird history to life-like reality. Rave reviews usually follow a visit to this attraction. Open daily May through October. Admission is $7.00 for those 12 years and up, $5.00 for those between 5 and 11 years old. Children under 5 years are admitted free.

DEER RANCH

(☎ 906.643.7760 ⌁ deerranch.com) Four miles west of the Mackinac Bridge is the oldest live whitetail deer exhibit in North America. Visitors are invited to photograph and feed the deer and fawns in their natural settings. A walking trail leads visitors past some of the deer's favorite spots. A large gift shop specializes in deer hide leather goods. Admission is $4.50 for everyone over 4 years old.

GARLYN ZOOLOGICAL PARK

(Hwy 2, Naubinway, MI ☎ 906.477.1085 ⌁ garlynzoo.com) This is a very special zoo that just keeps improving year after year. They started out with wild animals that they kept as pets and have moved into animal rescue. Bears, porcupines, cougars and peacocks live next to the camel and alligators. Each animal has its own habitat and is vigilantly monitored by zoo staff. They are open seven days a week from April until October. March and November are open for weekends only, weather permitting. Call ahead to verify available hours during these months. The rustic, natural garden setting promotes the authentic habitat desired for the best care of the animals. The gift shop offers educational materials, gifts and toys. An entire day could easily pass in this fascinating park. Admission prices are $8.00 for adults, $7.00 for children 3-16 years, under 3 years are free. A family pass for $28.00 covers the entrance cost of 6 people over the age of 3 years. Annual passes are available.

SOUTH MACKINAC

South of Mackinaw City, in areas such as **Indian River** and **Gaylord**, the opportunities for tourists increase. Each town adds its own touch to the tourism industry in Michigan. As the focus of this guide is on the Mackinac area, a few of the easiest to access and most enjoyable are included.

BIG BEAR ADVENTURES

(4271 S Straits Hwy ☎ *231.238.8181* ☝ *bigbearadventures.com)* The Sturgeon River is a lovely river for water adventures. The friendly owners of Big Bear Adventures have been bringing people together with the river for years. Sturgeon River Trips may be taken on canoe, kayak, raft, catamaran or tube. The necessary safety gear is included with the rental of the conveyance of your choice. The average water depth is three to four feet with pools that average five to eight feet. Rent fees include shuttle service to the starting point and from the ending point in Burt Lake State Park. Pricing begins with the minimum 1 ½ hour excursion at $10.00 per person for a tube and up to $19.00 per person for kayak. No experience necessary for this fun, wet adventure. They also have Adventure Miniature Golf and a combination General Store/Gift Shop. Winter adventures include snow shoeing and cross country skiing. Equipment for these activities is available for rent.

CROSS IN THE WOODS CATHOLIC SHRINE

(7078 M-68, Indian River ☎ *231.238.8181* ☝ *crossinthewoods.com)* Michigan's most visited shrine is open all year. They are home to the largest collection of dolls adorned with the traditional habits of the Catholic religious community. 525 dolls and 20 mannequins represent 217 orders. This is a fascinating collection to view even for those who are not of the Catholic faith. One lady is responsible for creating this collection and the attention to detail is inspiring. Outside of the Doll Museum and gift shop is the actual Cross in the Woods. The cross was erected in 1954. The corpus was added in 1959. Twenty-eight stairs leading up to the cross were added in 1956. Many pilgrims to the shrine ascend them during private prayer as they meditate the Passion of Christ. Five additional shrines to various saints nestle among the beautiful garden and woods. This is an active parish and guests are invited to join in the services. There is no admission fee, but they accept donations.

CALL OF THE WILD MUSEUM & BAVARIAN FALLS PARK

(850 S Wisconsin Ave. ☎ *989.732.4336* ✆ *gocallofthewild.com)* Life size displays showcase wildlife in their natural habitat. Hands-on activities are throughout the displays, which also teach about animal behaviors and habitats. This is not just for kids! These exhibits are captivating for all ages. The gift shop features quality items with a rustic, woodsy theme. Adjacent to the museum is the Bavarian Falls Park. Eighteen holes of miniature golf chart their course past streams, ponds and waterfalls. Go-Karts and Krazy Kars (bumper cars) use up energy before the one-hour drive back to Mackinaw City. The museum is open all year as is the gift shop. The Bavarian Falls Park closes when the snow flies and reopens in the spring as soon as the weather permits. Admission to the museum is $7.00 for adults, seniors at $6.50 and children ages 4-13 years for $4.50. From I-75, follow exit 282 east for 3 blocks then turn right on Wisconsin Avenue. It is 6 blocks to the museum.

Recommendations

As a family, we have visited Mackinaw City and Mackinac Island many times. Sometimes we went on business, other times for pleasure. The *Memorial Day Re-enactment at Colonial Michilimackinac* is the number one favorite in this household. Each year we trek into town for the parade before the show. The re-enactors march in the parade in character. The children always try to anticipate just when some of the Native American characters will break out and enter the crowd with their war whoops and raised tomahawks. We never guess it correctly.

A fashion show precedes the re-enactment at the fort. The costumes are historically correct and the fashion show gives each character type an opportunity to showcase their outfits. During the re-enactment, the loud speakers narrate the events. Some of the French is poorly pronounced, which drives me nuts. I can only imagine, based on the smothered giggles, how French speaking Canadians feel about it. I do hope they correct that. Pronunciation aside, the narration is accurate and easy to follow. The game played outside the fort as part of the presentation is the most exciting part. The players are skilled and give their all as they compete. My son dreams of joining in someday. He has a few years before he is old enough. My daughters are researching and sketching their costumes as British ladies. Perhaps they will side with the French ladies. They are keeping their options open.

Demonstrations and activities, especially the archaeological dig, fill the summer days at Colonial Michilimackinac. Anytime you go, something new is always ready to catch your attention. I count it as educational. They like to go and fire up their imaginations.

Sunday afternoons are a favorite time for us to stroll the *Mackinaw Crossings Mall* and *Central Avenue*. There are so many interesting shops to visit. People-watching is a fun pasttime as well. This is best accomplished with ice cream in hand. Sometimes I suspect that the ice cream is the best part. We try to finish our visit with a late afternoon climb up into the *lighthouse*. We count the lighthouses that we can see from here, knowing how many we should see. A freighter or two might catch our attention as well. These Ladies of the Lakes are the reason for much of the industry and economy in the states surrounding the Great Lakes. We enjoy seeing them whenever we can.

My children have visited several waterparks and always claim *Thunder Falls Water Park* as their favorite. The slides are bigger, faster. The wave pool is "the best." As a parent, I find that their safety precautions are superior to other fine parks that we have visited. The price is reasonable, too.

The *Mackinac Bridge* is the next item on my family's list. There are lots of bridges in the world, but this one is ours and we love it. Maybe it is just a Michigan thing, I don't know. A drive across the bridge always brings up feelings of adventure and anticipation. If we are headed into the Upper Peninsula, time on the *beach* is likely to happen.

Of course, the *Annual Labor Day Bridge Walk* has left a shining memory in each of us. The National Guard supervises from their placement at intervals across the bridge. Their vigilance is a necessary precaution. Thankfully, they have never had to use their training during this event. The people, the excitement, everything combines to make this a very special time.

Biking around Mackinac Island is exhilarating. It does not require much practice or experience to accomplish this feat. Plenty of resting stops encourage novices. There are just enough low hills to keep the interest of those with more expertise. Biking through the middle of the island is more challenging. The hills are steeper. The paths lead through forests, past streams and meadows. This is the path less taken and it amply rewards those who accept the challenge. There is a different kind of freedom in biking on Mackinac Island. It is an island, after all and no matter where you go, you can never really get lost. Stay the course and downtown will soon be in sight.

Downtown Mackinac Island is another excellent spot to people-watch. There are so many visitors from so many different places. Many languages can be overheard. Cultures do not collide here. They mingle and bring out the best in each other. The shops and art galleries are a draw all by themselves. An entire day is easily spent just browsing through them. My youngest sums it up, "Downtown is really cool."

The *stables at the Grand Hotel* are open to the public at no charge. They house thoroughbred horses that pull the carriages and dray carts for the Grand Hotel. A display gives background and insight into types of carriages used and why these particular horse breeds have been selected. Their tack room is well appointed. One visit never seems to satisfy.

In this technological age, we sometimes forget the joy of exploration. Peeking into caves, climbing among the rocks, and allowing ourselves to be fascinated by creation is a past time that needs to be deliberately cultivated. The rewards go far beyond the intellectual. They touch the imagination and stir our hearts as little else can do.

Sometimes we play "tourist" and visit the attractions and sights that we may otherwise overlook. Living in an area can tend to breed complacency towards the opportunities available. So we don our tourist hats and hit the road. We have discovered that tubing down the Sturgeon River is a necessary rite of summer, not just for visitors. Our opinions have been corrected as places that once were little nothing tourist traps have reinvented themselves into worthwhile stops.

Index

1

1852 Grill Room, 127

A

Admiral's Table, 121
America's Best Value Inn, 137
American Fur Company Store, 76
Anchor Budget Inn, 138
Anishinabe, 20
Anna's Buffet, 121
Antiques & Classics on the Bay, 66
Aqua-Grand Mackinaw Inn and Waterpark, 136
Arch Rock, 83
Arnold Line, 51
Astor Street Cafe, 127
Audie's Chippewa Room, 121

B

B.C. Pizza, 121
battlefield, the, 81
Bavarian Falls Park, 169
Bay Cottage, 153
Bay View at Mackinac, 154
Baymont Inn & Suites, 138
Beach House, The, 138
Beachcomber Motel, 138
beaches, 95
Beaumont Memorial, 76
Benjamin Blacksmith Shop, 77

Best Western Dockside Waterfront, 136
Best Western Thunderbird Inn, 139
bicycles, Mackinac Island, 61
Biddle House, 76
Big Bear Adventures, 168
Big Boy Restaurant, 122
bike tours, 66
Bistro on the Greens, 127
Blue Water Grill & Bar, 122
boat docks, Soo Locks, 160
boating, 101
Brigadoon Bed & Breakfast, 143
British Landing, 81
Budget Host American Boutique Inn, 139
bus, getting to Mackinaw by, 47
Butterfly House, 106

C

Call of the Wild Museum, 169
Canada Day Celebration, 67
Cannonball Drive-In, 127
canoeing, 101
Carlton's Tea Shop, 127
Carp Lake, 102
Carriage House, 127
carriage, Mackinac Island. *See* horse and carriage, Mackinac Island
Castle Rock, 164
Chateau Lorraine, 154
Chillin' and Grillin', 128
Chippewa Hotel Waterfront, 149

Cindy's Riding Stable.
Clarion Hotel Beachfront, 139
Cloghaun Bed and Breakfast, 154
Colonial Michilimackinac, 93
Colonial Michilimackinac Pageant, 65
Comfort Inn Lakeside, 139
Comfort Suites Lakeview, 136
Concerts on the Lawn, 97
Corvette Crossroads, 68
Cottage Inn of Mackinac, 154
Courtyard Inn & Suites, 140
Cross in the Woods, 168
Cudahy Room Inn, 128
Cunningham's Family Restaurant, 122

D

Darrow's Family Restaurant, 122
Days Inn Bridgeview, 140
Days Inn Lakeview, 140
Deer Ranch, 167
Deerhead Inn, 144
Devil's Kitchen, 84
Dining Room, Grand Hotel, 129
directions to Mackinaw, 46
Dixie Saloon, 123
Dog House, 128
Doud's Market, 128
Dream Seaker Charters and Tours, 165

E

Eastern Upper Peninsula Fishing Charters, 165
Econo Lodge At the Bridge, 140

Econo Lodge Bayview, 136
Embers Restaurant, 123
Epicurean, 128
Espresso Cafe, 128

F

Father Marquette National Park, 163
ferry, getting to Mackinac Island by, 49
Fine Arts & Crafts Show, 67
fishing, 101
Flamingo Motel, 140
Fort De Baude Museum, 164
Fort Holmes, 81
Fort Mackinac, 74
Fort Mackinac Tea Room, 129
Fred's Deli, 129
French Farm Lake, 101

G

Garlyn Zoological Park, 167
Gate House, 129
Gathering Place, The, 20
golf, 107
Goodfellows Grill, 129
Grand Hotel, 148
Grand View Resort, 141
Great Lakes Air, 164
Great Lakes Inn, 141

H

Hamilton Inn, 141
Hampton Inn, 141
Harbot View Dining, 130
Harbour View Inn, 150
Haunted Theatre, The, 107

Headlands, The, 99
Historic Depot, The, 123
Historic Mill Creek Discovery
    Park, 94
Holiday Inn Express, 141
Horn's Gaslight, 130
horse and carriage, Mackinac
    Island, 61
Hotel Iroquois, 150

I

Icebreaker Mackinaw Maritime
    Museum, 95
Indian Dormitory, 78
Inn at Stonecliffe, The, 152
Insect Museum, 106
Ironworkers Festival, 67
Island House Hotel, 150

J

Jack Pine Lumberjack Show, 97
Jack's Livery Stable, 62
Jewel, The, 107
JR.'s Tailgate Pub, 123

K

kayaking, 101
Kite Festival, 67

L

Lake View Hotel, 151
Lakeside Market, 130
Laser Light Show, 98
Lighthouse Restaurant, 123
Lilac Festival, 68
Lilac Tree Hotel and Spa, 151

Lower Peninsula, 43

M

M-185, 60
Mackinac Island Bike Shop, 61
Mackinac Island Carriage Tours,
    62
Mackinac Island State Dock, 51
Mackinac Old Time Trolley
    Company, 98
Mackinac State Historic Parks,
    74
Mackinaw Breeze Catamaran
    Sailing, 105
Mackinaw City KOA, 144
Mackinaw City Municipal
    Marina, 51
Mackinaw Club, 107
Mackinaw Pastie & Cookie Co.,
    124
Mackinaw Trolley Company
    Tours, 98
Mahdezewin International, 160
Main Street Inn, 152
Mama Mia's Pizzeria, 124
Mancino's of Mackinaw City, 124
Market Street Inn, 154
Martha's Sweet Shop, 130
Mary's Bistro, 130
Maze of Mirrors, 98
McGulpin House, 75
McGulpin Lighthouse, 100
Memorial Bridge Race, 65
Memorial Day Parade, 65
Mighty Mac Hamburgers, 131
Millie's on Main, 131
Mission Church, 78
Mission Point Resort, 149
Missionary Bark Chapel, 79

Murray Hotel, 152
Murray Hotel Lunch and Dinner
  Buffet, 131
Museum Ship Valley Camp, 161
Music in Mackinaw, 67

N

Neath the Birches, 124
Nona Lisa, 125
Northpointe Inn, 137

O

O'Reillys Irish Pub, 125
Odawa, 21
Old Mackinac Point Lighthouse,
  94
Orr Kid's Bike Shop, 61

P

Palace Restaurant, 125
Pancake Chef, 125
Pancake House, 131
Paradise Lake, 102
parasailing, 96
Parkside Inn, 142
pastie, 119
Patrick Sinclair's Irish Pub, 131
Pellston Regional Airport, 48
Pine Cottage, 154
Pink Pony Bar and Grill, 131
Point Lookout, 81
Post Cemetery, 80
Potawatomi, 20
Professor Harry's Old Time
  Photos, 106

Q

Quality Inn, 142

R

Rail Trail, Mackinaw City, 101
Ramada Inn, 142
River of History Museum, 161
Riviera Motel, 142
Round Island Bar & Grill, 132
Ryba's Bike Rental, 61

S

sand dunes, Lake Michigan, 166
Scalawags Whitefish & Chips,
  126
Seabiscuit, 132
Shepler's Ferry, 50
Shepler's Lighthouse Cruises, 96
shuttles, Mackinaw City, 53
Skull Cave, 84
Soo Locks, 159
St. Ignace Car Show, 67
Star Line, 50
Ste. Anne's Church, 80
Straits of Mackinac, The, 42
Straits Underwater Dive
  Preserve, 166
Sugar Loaf Rock, 83
Super 8 Motel Beachfront, 143
Super 8 Motel Bridgeview, 143
Survey Monument of Michigan,
  160

T

Tee Pee Campground, 144
Three Brothers Sarducci, 132

Three Fires, The, 19
Thunder Falls Waterpark, 96
Tower of History, 161
transportation, Mackinaw City, 52
transportation, winter, Mackinac Island, 53
Trappers Creek Adventure Golf, 99
Trinity Episcopal Church, 79
Two Amigos, 123

U

Upper Peninsula, 43

V

Vesper Cruise, 66
Village Inn, 132

W

walking, Mackinaw City, 52
Water Street Historical Block, 162
Waugoshaunce Point, 100
Wawashkamo Golf Club, 108
Weird Michigan Wax Museum, 166
Wilderness State Park, 100
Windermere Hotel, 153
Wings of Mackinac, 106
winter transportation. *See* transportation, winter, Mackinac Island
Woods, 132

Y

Yankee Rebel Tavern, 132

ABOUT THE AUTHOR

Donna Marie Lively is a lifelong fan of the Mackinac area. She has lived in both peninsulas and currently resides in Petoskey, Michigan. Donna and her husband own businesses in both the Upper Peninsula and northern Lower Peninsula of Michigan. They have found that home schooling their children allows them ample opportunities to experience northern Michigan and especially the Mackinac area. Donna is a graduate of Eastern Michigan University where she specialized in children's literature, science and pedagogy. In addition to her interest in the Mackinac area, Donna enjoys historical research, exploring, archery, and needlecrafts.

NOTES:

NOTES:

NOTES:

NOTES:

NOTES:

TOURIST TOWN GUIDES™

Explore America's
Fun Places

Books in the *Tourist Town Guides*™ series are available at book-stores and online. You can also visit our website for additional book and travel information. The address is:

http://www.touristtown.com

Black Hills
($14.95, ISBN 978-0-9792043-1-9)

Breckenridge
($14.95 ISBN 978-0-9767064-9-6)

Frankenmuth
($13.95, ISBN 978-0-9767064-8-9)

Hershey
($13.95, ISBN 978-0-9792043-8-8)

Key West, 2nd Edition
($14.95, ISBN 978-1-935455-02-8)

Mackinac
($14.95, ISBN 978-0-9767064-7-2)

Ocean City
($13.95, ISBN 978-0-9767064-6-5)

Also Available:
(See touristtown.com for details)

Atlantic City
Gatlinburg
Jackson Hole
Las Vegas
Myrtle Beach
Niagara Falls
Wisconsin Dells

TOURIST TOWN GUIDES™
www.touristtown.com

ORDER FORM #1
ON REVERSE SIDE

Tourist Town Guides™ is published by:

Channel Lake, Inc.
P.O. Box 1771
New York, NY 10156

TOURIST TOWN GUIDES™
ORDER FORM

Telephone: With your credit card handy,
call toll-free 800.592.1566

Fax: Send this form toll-free to 866.794.5507

E-mail: Send the information on this form
to orders@channellake.com

Postal mail: Send this form with payment to Channel Lake, Inc.
P.O. Box 1771, New York, NY, 10156

Your Information: ( ) Do not add me to your mailing list

Name: _____

Address: _____

City: _____ State: _____ Zip: _____

Telephone: _____

E-mail: _____

Book Title(s) / ISBN(s) / Quantity / Price
(see previous pages or www.touristtown.com for this information)

_____

_____

_____

Total payment*: $_____

Payment Information: (Circle One)   Visa / Mastercard

Number: _____ Exp: _____

Or, make check payable to: **Channel Lake, Inc.**

* Add the lesser of $6.50 USD or 18% of the total purchase price for shipping. International orders call or e-mail first! New York orders add 8% sales tax.

TOURIST TOWN GUIDES™

www.touristtown.com

ORDER FORM #2
ON REVERSE SIDE

(for additional orders)

Tourist Town Guides™ is published by:

CHANNEL LAKE, INC.
Book Publisher

Channel Lake, Inc.
P.O. Box 1771
New York, NY 10156

▐TOURIST TOWN▌ GUIDES™
ORDER FORM

Telephone: With your credit card handy,
call toll-free 800.592.1566

Fax: Send this form toll-free to 866.794.5507

E-mail: Send the information on this form
to orders@channellake.com

Postal mail: Send this form with payment to Channel Lake, Inc.
P.O. Box 1771, New York, NY, 10156

Your Information: ( ) Do not add me to your mailing list

Name: _____

Address: _____

City: _____ State: _____ Zip: _____

Telephone: _____

E-mail: _____

Book Title(s) / ISBN(s) / Quantity / Price
(see previous pages or www.touristtown.com for this information)

_____

_____

_____

Total payment*: $_____

Payment Information: (Circle One)   Visa / Mastercard

Number: _____ Exp: _____

Or, make check payable to: **Channel Lake, Inc.**

* Add the lesser of $6.50 USD or 18% of the total purchase price for shipping. International orders call or e-mail first! New York orders add 8% sales tax.